LOSING A SON, FINDING MYSELF

Mike Horton

© Copyright 2015 By Mike Horton
ISBN: 1508481466
ISBN 13: 9781508481461

For my "Bee"

FOREWORD

"The result of Mike Horton's emotional and sincere re-living of Alan's death is now where it belongs, in the hands of the reader.

Mike has held back nothing while relating to you his deepest thoughts.

Every paragraph, sentence, and word was written after prayer and what had to be divine inspiration.

If this book in any way helps you to ease your suffering or encourages you to find comfort in your faith and to continue to live the precious gift of life that God has given to you, I think that will be your ultimate gift to the memory of your loved one.

If this beautiful book only helps one person, this book will have achieved its purpose, and Mike Horton has honored Alan's memory."

—Peggy Andersen Conard Thompson

PREFACE

I didn't want to write this book. Then, I didn't want to stop writing this book. It was completed months ago. I told my friends I was fine-tuning the acknowledgements page. I realized I was stalling. In a way, it would signal the end of a relationship I have had with the chronicling of my child's life. For two years I have dedicated myself to this project. Now, it's done. It's time to let go and share Alan with the rest of the world as Ellis Amburn put it so eloquently.

I had two goals in mind when I began writing. To honor my son, and to share my hope with other parents; especially fathers who have lost a child and who might be considering taking their own life—like my brother, Terry, did when he lost his precious 3 year-old daughter, Kim. It took him 30 years to drink himself to death.

Fr. Ron Rolheiser referred to the death of a child as the only unnatural death there is. It is out of sequence. It's not supposed to happen, and it is not fair. In the course of my writings and research, I have concluded that being a suck-it-up-and-go-tough kind of guy, is not just a "Texas thing," it's across the board. Black, white, brown, it doesn't matter. Men just don't share. We keep it inside like a ticking time bomb until it takes toll on our health, our marriages; even on our very lives itself.

If you are a parent in despair over the loss of your child, and are considering suicide, I implore you to get help. There are hotlines and agencies available to help you through this. GriefShare, Compassionate Friends, church groups. Anything, other than turning to that final option. There is a Heaven and we will see our children again.

ACKNOWLEDGEMENTS

I'd like to thank those who have so graciously given of their time and talent to help make this work of love a reality. Donna Foti Horton, thank you for being the great mom that you are and for helping to raise three wonderful kids. As you say, "We have one in Gainesville, one in LA, and one in Heaven. Anna Horton, your talents as an artist, proofreader, and designer, have produced a handsome cover for your brother's book. Thank you for the endless hours of love and dedication you put into this project. Austin James Horton at least half of Alan's nine lives can be attributed to your guardianship. Thanks for watching over him. Yesenia Vera, thank you for the timeless photo that graces our front cover. Gayle Horton PhD. You said, "You should write a book." And so I did. Thank you for your confidence, love, and editing skills. Gayle Kotin Stein, Peggy Andersen Conard Thompson, and Lois Celli Redford. You were the "writing coaches," that got me through these past two years. I will never forget your love and dedication. Ellis Amburn you taught me the discipline of good writing. Pedro Hernandez, Beatrice Solis, and Gilbert Guzman. Thank you for your Spanish translation help. Richard Lee Hall, you are most definitely, "the man." Kaye Linden, for Createspace and Amazon.com, I am forever grateful. Fr. Emmanuel Pazhayapurackal, Carlos and Margarita Barzaga, Cecily Wilson Henderson, Susan Wilson Oakley, Dr. Bob Oakley, Spirit Wind Ministry, Don and Corky, M.J. and Gini Stirna, Paula D'Arcy, God bless you. Linda Harding, Rick Wulff, Jean Fish, Ginny Pemberton, and all of my friends at the Saturday morning group. Lastly, "Heartspeak," is a foundation I've established to help grieving parents to help one another. It can be found on Facebook. God bless us and our children.

CHAPTER ONE

"Look, you need to make a decision. Your son is never going to wake up."

I stand paralyzed, feeling as if a hole has just been blown through my chest by a double-barreled shotgun.

The doctor who had just saved my son from cardiac arrest tells me, "If he arrests one more time, we won't be able to save his organs. That's what you told me he wanted, right?"

The doctor wheels around and leaves. I try to wrap my mind around the surreal events of the last few hours. My 25-year old son, Alan, has just sustained terrible injuries after falling from a two-story ladder. He will never again regain consciousness. If he survives, he will live in a vegetative state—and I know he wouldn't want that. Now it is up to me to decide his fate. But all systems shut down as I refuse to accept the reality of this situation. He'll never laugh and sing, make funny drawings, attend nursing school, or call me for advice about life, love or business dealings. He'll never again say, "Love you, Dad."

"I love you too, my Bee." I hear myself say as I slump against the hospital wall, rocked to the foundation of my soul.

Alan is terminally comatose, and likely facing another heart attack. He is in danger of being denied the last wish of his generous soul—that his organs be donated to help save lives.

Finding my way to his bedside, I put my head on his chest, wrap my arms around him, and weep. I am trying to pour every ounce of love I possess out of my heart into his. I sense he knows what I am doing. Though usually surrounded by his mother, Donna, his older brother, Austin, his sister, Anna, or his girlfriend, Yesenia Vera (Jessie), the room has cleared and we are alone.

I hold him for a long time with my face pressed to his chest, listening to his strong heartbeat. How much longer, I wonder. How much longer do we have?

I realize this could be the last time I'd ever be alone with my son. How on earth am I going to be able to decide whether he lives or dies?

I recall the Terri Schiavo case that gained national attention in 2005. It was the seven-year legal battle to take a Florida woman in a persistent vegetative state off life support. Her husband had filed a petition in opposition to her parents' belief that she was still conscious.

Terri had suffered a full cardiac arrest and incurred massive brain damage from oxygen depletion. She remained comatose for two and a half months before doctors declared her vegetative. She then lay in a coma for 15 years.

Though efforts to terminate life support were opposed by President George W. Bush, her feeding tube was eventually removed by court order. She died two weeks later on March 31, 2005.

I can't allow this to happen to my son. Although he looks as if he is only asleep, I know he's not going to wake up. He's not dead, but exactly where is he?

A Life Alliance Organ Recovery Agency (LAORA) representative asks to meet with the family. Austin, Anna, Donna, my wife Gayle, and I meet her in the conference room. Jessie joins us after a few minutes. Alan's driver's license identifies him as an organ donor.

"Oh, no, no, no," Jessie interjects. "He was going to change that. That's not what he wanted at all. That's wrong."

The kind and compassionate rep looks perplexed.

Jessie alone witnessed Alan's fall. She's still in shock, even denying that we're doing everything possible to save his life. The fact remains that Alan had chosen to be an organ donor. It is a decision his mother and I will honor.

God, please let this be the right decision.

Memories spring up of the father-son trip we took to the Grand Canyon in 2008. I treated each one of my children to a vacation in the Southwestern desert of New Mexico, the Grand Canyon, Sedona, Bell Rock, and Tucson. We'd always end up at my niece Susie's in Rockport, Texas for a Fourth of July party and fireworks show. In 2004, I took Austin, Anna in 2007, and I was about to take Alan in 2008, but he was unpredictable. I loved him dearly but it was virtually impossible to get him away from Jessie. She rarely let him out of her sight.

I love Jessie to this day, but I never understood why Alan never wanted to leave her. Gayle said it was all about the chicken soup. When they'd first met, Alan became very ill, and it was Jessie who nursed him back to health. "She was the mommy who would never abandon him."

I needed reassurance he wasn't going to be a no-show.

"Okay, now, Bee," I cautioned over the phone, "I'm going to reserve tickets for our flights and set up our car rentals. You know you've got to be here in Gainesville on the 26th of June, right?"

"Yeah, Dad."

"Bee, you can't miss our departure date. The tickets are non-refundable."

"No problemo."

"I've got a few grand into this, son. You *will* be on the bus tomorrow, right?"

"Yes, but of course, Dad-ee-oh."

"Bee, I'm hanging up now. I'll see you in the morning at 10:30, okay?"

"Yeah. I'll be there, Dad."

"Love you much, my Bee. Have a good trip up from Miami."

"Okay, Dad. Love you too."

I wasn't sure he'd make it, but I prayed that he'd show up, and he did. Stepping off the bus, he had a smile as big as Texas. He was the last of my kids to make the "Horton Desert Sojourn", a summertime tradition started by my father decades ago.

In Albuquerque, Alan and I rented a sleek silver Dodge Challenger with XM satellite radio. We both loved oldies. Singing along to "Runaway" and "Unchained Melody" we barrel across the desert towards Santa Fe. The Tokens' "The Lion Sleeps Tonight" was Alan's favorite oldies song.

From Santa Fe we headed west through the Painted Desert and stopped at Meteor City to check out the souvenir shop. I was inspecting hats and t-shirts when he came running up to me with an envelope in his hand.

"Dad, look! Rattlesnake eggs."

I opened the flap as something loud hissed and snapped inside the envelope. I screamed and jumped a foot in the air before realizing it was only a toy rattler attached to a coiled rubber band. Alan was beside himself laughing. A seasoned trickster, he was the master of practical jokes.

At sunset we arrived at the Grand Canyon and checked into our hotel. After dinner we fired up Alan's laptop and watched movies together on the floor like we did when he was little. The next morning we were up at 4:30. We made it to the South Rim just in time to catch the sunrise.

Alan captured the exact moment the sun peeked out over the canyon wall. It was a majestic sight. He saw beauty in everything, and was truly a gifted photographer. As we hiked along the canyon, he'd stop to photograph even the tiniest wildflower.

In Sedona, Alan added his name to the spot on Bell Rock where Austin and Anna had carved their names years before. Every place of interest along the highway was recorded with stunning photography. Many of his pictures Gayle had matted and framed. Today, they adorn the walls of our home.

I study Alan's face as he now lies in the hospital bed, thanking God for our desert trek that we had shared. His eyes now look tired and weary. How could I let him become a prisoner inside a body kept alive by machines? Caressing his face, I begin to cry.

"I love you my Bee, and I'll see you again someday, my sweet child."

I turn to Donna and say, "We have to honor his wish. I don't want to keep him from moving on."

She agrees. I cross the ward floor to longtime family friend, Bruce Howland. Though the fury of a supernova is exploding within my soul, I manage to get out the words, "We're going to let him go" before I lose it. Screaming, "Oh, God!" I collapse into Bruce. Standing tall, he grabs me to his chest to muffle my cries and drags me to the conference room. I don't remember anything else.

Life Alliance Organ Recovery Agency initiates the procedure to procure Alan's organs. The "harvesting," as LAORA calls it, will occur the next day. That's supposed to give us time to say goodbye.

I collapse on the conference room floor where we'd been camped out since our arrival. Gayle is with me. Austin and Anna are nearby. I didn't know I could cry so hard or for so long. The sorrow of every loss I've ever experienced in my life combined together doesn't even come close to this.

Someone once told me that when God opens the gates of Heaven, the first ones in are parents who've lost children. I pray that's true. I try to stay awake and let scenes from my lifetime with Alan fill my mind.

CHAPTER TWO

At age five Alan attended the Jewish Community Center in Miami Beach. His teacher, Miss Sophie, who was like a "Bubbie" to him, taught him a Hebrew blessing that he loved to recite before dinner. One night he asked, "Dad, are we Jewish?"

Smiling, I answered, "Well, kind of Bee. Our Catholic religion originated in Judaism."

"So, I'll be going to Temple Beth Sholom?"

"No, Alan, I'm pretty sure you'll be going to Saint Patrick's."

His sister often felt protective of him when they were growing up. Anna recalls, "Alan was just a skinny little boy with big glasses. He was so precious, nerdy, and good-natured, I worried he might not be able to defend himself out there in the real world.

Of course, in middle school that all changed," she adds. "He met the twins—Armando and Enrique—and the three became inseparable. Together, they would work out, grow strong, get into mischief, and have each other's backs. Even though Bee got tougher on the outside, his heart never hardened."

Enrique was always impressed with Alan's climbing skills. "He could go straight up a 30'-40' coconut tree with only his hands." Chuckling, he continues, "...and that boy did have some big hands. He won twenty bucks once on a dare from some guy who challenged him to pick a coconut. 'Show me the money,' Alan said. The guy did. Alan laughed, grabbed the bill, and was up and down the tree in less than a minute with a big green coconut in his hand. The dude couldn't believe what he just saw. We laughed our asses off at that guy. We all knew better. Alan was like a native islander. He was awesome to watch."

Alan was strong and he was also built for speed. On the varsity football team at Southwest High, he was a defensive safety and nobody got past him. Alan and the twins called themselves "The Three Musketeers." Armando recalls Alan's zest for life.

"Alan lived life to the fullest."

However, there were times Alan pushed the envelope too far. He got into partying so much that the twins had to tell him to slow down and back off a bit. Once, Alan got kicked out of a friend's house after getting caught by their mom with girls and pot. I'm embarrassed to admit that he learned a lot of these things from me.

When Alan was 16, I had a reaction I attributed to PTSD from an earlier traumatic event in my life. In one week: I bought three cars, a new BMW motorcycle, put money down on a 1929 Waco biplane allegedly flown by Charles Lindbergh, and almost closed on a guest house in Key West. Alan was my partner-in-crime back then. Driving around smoking weed and listening to reggae music, we bonded deeply. I even took him to Tootsie's, an upscale gentlemen's club in Miami. Although not exactly Ward Cleaver material, Alan thought I was the coolest dad on Earth.

Thrilling as it was, my PTSD adventure had been but a brief departure in my long tenure as a responsible parent. Enrique reminded me,

"You know back in the eighth grade when you separated us for smoking pot—"

"I separated you guys?"

"Yeah. It was the best thing you ever did. It made me realize I was messing up my own family and screwing up my life. I had to reassess my relationship with my own folks because of you separating us, Mr. Horton. At first I thought, 'Whoa, why is Mr. Horton bein' such an asshole, man?' But then I realized you were doing it to protect Alan. We were apart for almost an entire year. Until we played football together at Southwest, you didn't let us hang out."

I knew that would have been tough, because "The Three Musketeers" had been together constantly since they met. Enrique told me I had been a good father figure to both him and Armando. He moved me to tears when he revealed, "You made a big difference in our lives when we were growing up, Mr. Horton."

I blame myself for Alan's excessive pot use. Maybe if I hadn't taken him on that PTSD "rocket ride," he wouldn't have smoked pot everyday. I discover this when the LAORA staff inquires about recreational drug use. Jessie tells them.

"We smoked every day,"

"Every day, Jessie?" I'm crestfallen. "Was he smoking the morning he went up on the ladder?"

"Yes, but it was hours earlier."

Austin assures us that Alan could always handle his pot. After all, he ran a successful business and he was on the Dean's List every semester in college.

I disagree. I had followed Alan once when I knew he'd been smoking. He was driving so erratically I was sure he was going to crash. He had already wrecked the car I bought him, his mother's car, Jessie's car, and her father's truck.

Armando sides with Austin, "It wasn't due to smoking pot, Mr. Horton. We were all smoking huge amounts of weed back then, and Alan could always handle it."

But he'd totaled four cars.

In the conference room at Ryder Trauma Center I try to sleep but can't. I keep waking up fearing that they are going to remove Alan from the ward without telling me. I'm hyper-vigilant. I'm aware the time with my son is limited.

The surgery to recover Alan's organs is scheduled for 11 a.m. tomorrow morning. We are fulfilling his wish to provide organs for people awaiting life-saving transplants. Unfortunately, this operation will also be ending his life.

Everyone is convinced he's comatose and is no longer responsive or truly "here". However, I sense his soul is still near. He is just beyond the veil that separates life from death, lingering and watching us, maintaining a tenuous connection to his still living body.

The LAORA rep briefs us on the protocol. Following surgery, Alan's body will be draped with a white shroud and adorned with a single long-stemmed red rose. It will then be taken from the hospital to the medical examiner's office.

Looking at my watch, I know time is running out. There are only a few hours left to hold his hand and sneak a few dozen more kisses onto his handsome face.

His older brother Austin cries out, "The wrong son is dying!"

"Austin, don't say that. This was an accident."

"Dad, I'd gladly trade places with Bee."

I hug him tight, and Anna joins in. We form a "love clump", embracing each other.

"I know you'd trade places with Alan, and he knows that too, Austin. Trust me, somehow he knows."

Classmates, friends, clients, and teachers show up. Sally, who taught Anna and Austin at St. Patrick's School in Miami Beach, is here. Alan had also worked on her house, and it was the townhouse down the street from hers where the accident happened. We are sobbing in each other's arms. She is completely devastated over his fall.

The Vera family arrives in full force. Jessie has been unable to leave his side for more than a few minutes. Her mother, Gilda, and her father Armando, are continuously with her. Armando speaks little English, but his love for Alan is apparent. He stands in silence and gazes at him lovingly. They had grown close during the years that Alan lived with Jessie at her parents' house. Alan worked hard to save money and he helped put Jessie through school. By scalping tickets to a music festival, he earned $30,000 for himself. Eventually, they were able to move into a fashionable high-rise in downtown Miami.

Alan once told me how he'd triumphantly grown a couple of papaya trees at the side of Jessie's house. Excited, he'd brag to me, "Dad, there's papayas all over!" He could grow anything, and was always interested in flowers and plants. He often asked Gayle for gardening tips, such as how to propagate roses from cuttings, and he'd follow through her instructions successfully. All his life he had retained that sense of wonder.

I loved his knack for coming up with strange statements and rhetorical questions. As a young child, he'd spring them on me at bedtime. When he was about four, I would lay next to him telling bedtime stories and trying to keep myself awake. That was usually when his revelations started.

"Dad?"

"Yes, Bee?"

"God never throws up."

There was a long silence as I struggled to get my mind around his observation. Was I supposed to answer this?
"Yes, Bee. I believe you're right about that."
"Even if he ate all the candy in the world?"
"Um, yeah. I guess so."
"But if he did he could make it disappear, right?"
"Yeah, probably Bee. Now, look. You need to go to sleep."
"Okay, Dad. Love you. 'Night."
"Goodnight, my Bee." I'd kiss him goodnight.
"Dad?"
"Yes, Bee?"
"Could you tell me a Timmy story? At this point, Austin and Anna would chime in from nearby.
"Yes, Dad. Please tell us a Timmy story."
"Okay, but just one. I mean it."
"Timmy stories" were my own invention. The main character was a fictional boy who'd get into predicaments and choose right from wrong. They were based largely on the series of Goofus and Gallant, characters from *Highlights Magazine for Children*. Usually told in a hypnotic monotone, they helped me to lull the kids to sleep. Sometimes the technique would backfire though, and the storyteller would wake up at 2 a.m. still in his shirt and tie.

As a single parent back then and after a long day at the office, cooking, cleaning, and setting up uniforms for the next day, I'd be toast by ten o'clock. Still, I'd do my best to put a coherent story line together. Fatigued and drifting into semi-consciousness, I'd garble something out like, "And then the dog pie ate the cyclone fence and…" Squeals of laughter would erupt from my kids. I think they loved my woozy alpha-state-babblings more than the stories themselves.

CHAPTER THREE

We gather around Alan. Austin is at the head of the bed stroking his brother's hair. The rest of us stare in silence at our young prince, who looks as if he'd just fallen asleep.

"Dad, we need to save a lock of Alan's hair."

Without a word, Gayle slips away and returns with scissors and small plastic bags. Austin tenderly clips a lock of Alan's curly brown hair for each of us. Now, we all have a part of him with us.

Soon, they will be here to take him from us. I'm on one side of his bed and Donna is on the other. Anna is folded in under my arm like a baby bird. Gayle is close by me. The Howland-Cook family, a number of friends and close relatives have filled the room.

I try to think only of my son, but my mind is teeming with images and words from the past. Especially my father reciting a line from Poe's "Annabel Lee", "…her highborn kinsmen came and bore her away from me".

Fifteen minutes remain. What the hell can I do in 15 minutes? Have I said enough prayers? Hugged and kissed him enough? I look back and forth at my kids and my wife as if they could tell me. My heart and soul implode in a black hole that swallows up every shred of light.

"They're ready for you now," a nurse announces.

I feel like I'm on death row being led to the gallows, scrambling for last words. I look at my watch again. A few minutes remain to search the faces of those around his bedside. Search for what? Could some miracle occur like Christ bringing Lazarus forth from the tomb?

Everything has been done. I know in my heart that I've never missed an opportunity to shower this child with love and affection. I have always been here for him. I've attended every school play, football game, and Cub Scout meeting. I was even there to help mend his broken heart after his first love ended.

When he was 17, he called to tell me his girl, Rosie, had broken up with him. He was still at her parents' house in Boca Raton. I could tell by his voice he was upset. She'd been the love of his life. They'd known each other since childhood. I was sad too. I believed they'd one day marry and have kids. After the breakup, Alan lingered at Rosie's for three days, stuck without a ride home. He was hanging on hoping for a reconciliation that wasn't going to happen.

"You need to get out of there," I urged him. "I'll pick you up in 45 minutes." When I arrived, Alan was standing alone in the front yard, wiping the tears streaming from his eyes. It was the only time in my life I'd ever seen my boy cry and it broke my heart.

Driving away from her house, I took Highway A1A back to Miami. The scenic route would give us more time to talk. I sat silently waiting for Alan to speak.

"I didn't see this coming," he said, "I just can't believe it's happening."

Rosie had made the decision to end the relationship.

"I'm so sorry this is happening to you," I empathized. "I know well the heartache of losing your first love. It's excruciating and I wish I could say there's a shortcut, but I've found the only way around pain is through it son. You think you'll never get over this feeling of your heart being crushed, but you will. Time will help you heal and someday, you *will* be happy again."

I turned into a parking lot facing the Atlantic so we could take a walk on the beach. Strolling past a couple of cute girls sunbathing, I had an idea. I pulled out a $20 and dared him to take off his shirt, walk over to the girls and ask for a phone number. His chiseled good looks and charming personality would certainly win the day. He snapped the bill up and headed toward the girls. A few minutes later he returned, grinning, and waving a piece of paper. I knew he was on the mend when he exclaimed, "Got it, Dad."

It occurs to me that God might take Alan before the doctors have the opportunity to remove his organs. I've always encouraged my son. Now it's in a way I have never anticipated. Leaning over, crying, I speak softly into his ear, "Just go to sleep, Baby. It's okay, my Bee. The angels will take you." I lower my head onto his chest to listen to his heartbeat. It is pounding strong as ever. He is still the boy who never gives up.

" Mr. Horton? "

Startled, I turn to see the nurse who is here to facilitate the transfer of Alan from ICU to the operating room.

CHAPTER FOUR

The eleventh hour has finally arrived. I feel my body changing as my sympathetic nervous system kicks in, pumping adrenaline and preparing me for what is to come: the long walk that will culminate in the death of Alan Michael Horton.

The priest who had administered the Last Sacraments to Alan prays for him and the family. At Gayle's request, he also blesses the doctors who will perform the transplant surgeries and prays that those receiving Alan's organs might live.

We stand aside as a team of nurses and technicians secure life-support equipment to his bed to ensure a continual flow of oxygen and medication during the transport process. It is a complex procedure. The operating room is across the hospital and on another floor. That is fine by me. Every minute is precious, and the more time I have with my son, the better.

I assume that only family makes the final walk, but the nurse tells me it's okay for others to come too. I look around at the faces of those who were standing by and praying for Alan. They have been here the past four days through the whole crisis. I am sharing his final moments with everyone he loved. They are around the ICU, in the conference room, in the hallway, and the visitor's area. Now they join the family in a procession that quickly becomes a massive display of love.

Donna and I take our usual positions on either side of Alan, Austin and Anna also cling to him. The nurse leads our entourage away from the ICU and down the hall. Gayle is beside me. Jessie, Bruce and Leilani, Armando and Enrique, Suzanne, Jason, and many others begin walking and weeping.

I feel my heart pulsating, blood is rushing so fast I can hear it in my head. "The Lord is my shepherd, I shall not want," I pray, and try to keep my composure as we all twist and turn through one hallway after another. A rapid-fire slide show of my son's life begins to play out in my mind. Christmas, the mini-bike we built together, fishing on the beach, playing in the tree house with Austin and Anna, all his birthday parties…

"Yea, though I walk through the valley of the shadow of death…" The doors of the operating room stand before us at the end of the hallway. I hold on tightly to Alan's hand as we come to a stop. The nurse who's accompanying us turns and says, "I'll give you a couple of minutes with Alan before I take him in." We all begin wailing so loudly that even the families of the organ recipients waiting in an adjoining room can hear us. They know someone has to die for these organs to become available.

Gayle walks into the waiting area to see which family's loved one will receive the gift of life. The LAORA rep had told her one recipient would be a middle-aged Hispanic male, a husband and a father. She scans the room until her eyes meet those of a Hispanic woman with young children. Wondering if this could be the receiving family, Gayle cries. These little children now have the chance to grow up with their daddy. She sees the love and hope that is in their eyes, and is reassured that Alan's sacrifice will make a difference in the lives of this family.

"The Blessed Mother and God's angels are with you," I promise Alan. "We'll all be together again someday in Heaven. I love you, Bee."

Gayle, Austin, Anna, Donna, and all the rest who'd accompanied us to the end of Alan's journey pray fervently. The doors swing open, and another nurse appears, one much less kind and tactful.

"I'm sorry," she says abruptly. "We have to take him to surgery now."

Another nurse pushes his bed away, and everyone sobs. I hold onto Alan, kissing him and hugging him, frantically grasping his hand until he is forcibly taken away. I shout out, "I love you, Bee! I love you, my baby, I love you forever!"

My last glimpse of Alan Michael Horton is of him being taken through those double doors. As they slowly close I cry, "Oh, my God. No. Please. No." The hammer of Almighty God swings down and shatters my heart and soul into a million pieces. Now...my son is gone.

CHAPTER FIVE

This crisis had begun days earlier. Gayle and I had just returned from our morning walk. It was 10:30 a.m. on October 19, 2010.

My cell phone goes off and as I look at the caller I.D. I can feel my body tense up. It's Donna, my children's mother. I turn to Gayle and say, "Uh oh, something must be wrong. Donna never calls at this time of the morning." We'd been divorced over 20 years.

"Hey Don. What's up?"

"Mike, Alan's had an accident. He fell from a ladder. They're airlifting him to Ryder Trauma Center in Miami."

"Oh, my God. What happened?" I begin shaking as I try to focus on her words.

"All I know is that Jessie said it's serious. He was up on a two-story ladder and he fell. I'm leaving in half an hour and driving straight down."

"Donna, please let me ride with you. I can be at your house in twenty minutes." She agrees.

I don't need to explain anything to Gayle, who is already packing my luggage carrier. I've barely hung up when the second call comes.

Jessie is crying hysterically. I can barely understand what she's saying. What I hear is:

"Mike, Mike, Alan's dead. Mike, he's dead!"

I fall to my knees, clutching Gayle. "Oh, my God," I cry out. "Not my baby! He's dead?"

Jessie corrects me. "No, Mike, he's not dead. I said, 'It's bad. It's bad.' Alan is being airlifted to the hospital. I'm on my way there now."

A million thoughts flood my mind. Why would this happen now? At 25 years of age, he's survived a wild life and is doing well as a nursing student in college. An artist and photographer, he's in his prime. Alan has been an expert climber all his life and a natural athlete, as agile as a cat. But somehow the child who never fell had fallen. I immediately call Ryder Trauma Center and inquire about his status.

"Mr. Horton, he is in the intensive care unit and he is in critical condition. That's all we can tell you right now. Please drive safely." I tell them I'll continually check in from the road and we'd arrive in Miami at 5:30 p.m. I ask them to call if they have any new information.

It has happened. The call that every parent is terrified of receiving, the one that informs you that something bad has happened to your child. Other people get those phone calls, not me. That happens to other families, other children, not mine. We take them into our arms at birth. We hold their hands when crossing the street. We get them water-safe and then teach them how to ride a bike without training wheels. We get them through driver's ed. and licensed. And then we pray, as they drive off on their own, that God will protect them from drunk drivers. We shield them for as long as we can and then we are supposed to let them go.

As a baby, Alan was an adventurer. One night after putting him to bed, I watched through a slightly opened door as he climbed out of his crib (not an easy feat as the sides were fairly high). He seemed so determined, as if he were making an escape from Alcatraz. He reached the floor just in time for me to pick him up and put him back. I watched again, amazed at his persistence and tenacity as he proceeded to repeat the maneuver. When he touched down, I retrieved him again, figuring I'd let him keep going until he tired. After doing this 19 times, I gave up. He showed no signs of slowing down. I knew *this* one was going to give me a run for the money.

Another time, I was looking out of our bedroom window on Miami Beach and marveling at the blue sky and coconut trees in our back yard. Suddenly, I froze as my gaze fell on the swing set. There, eight feet in the air, was my two-year-old son, Alan. He'd removed his diaper and was crawling naked across the monkey bars, having a blast. I ran out and coaxed him back to safety. As soon as he was within reach I snatched him up and handed him down to his very relieved mommy. He was smiling and hugging everybody. It was virtually impossible to get upset with him.

One day I was getting ready for work when I heard a loud knock on the front door. A smartly dressed woman held Alan out to Donna and me and said, "Excuse me. Is this your child?"

"Alan! How'd you get out of the house?"

Willie, the yardman next door, had seen him toddling down Post Avenue and given him to the elegant lady. I thanked her and explained that Alan must have used a chair on a box to reach the lock and slide bolt. He had watched me lock up the night before and figured it out.

Bee could solve just about anything, even as a baby. Once we got our baby safe in our arms, we went into shock at the possibility of a car hitting him, and we broke down crying. I immediately put a locking hook and eyelet on the outside of his bedroom door. I was determined there'd be no more chances of losing him.

As Gayle now drives me to Donna's, I pray for a miracle. Our family has had many. When my older sister, Rosemary, suffered a grand-mal seizure as a young child, Mom implored the Blessed Mother to heal her. She promised to recite the rosary every day for the rest of her life in return. The seizure stopped immediately. Rosemary never had another, and true to her word, Mom prayed the rosary every day.

When Rosemary's two-year-old granddaughter, Erin, fell out of a second-story window head first onto the concrete below, she was airlifted to a hospital and survived. We had all prayed for miracles and received them. Surely the same mercy would be granted to Alan.

When we park in front of Donna's house, I get out and assure Gayle that I'll call her with updates. Donna's boyfriend, Ed, insists that we take his brand-new SUV.

"I want to make sure you get to Miami safe and sound. Get going. I'll talk to you later."

We throw our luggage carriers in back, and head south out of Gainesville toward Florida's Turnpike.

Donna and I travel in complete silence. No radio, no sound other than the barely audible hum of tires on asphalt. This is the first time we've been alone together since our bitter divorce. None of that matters to me now as I focus all of my attention on our son.

I begin reciting my rosary, praying Alan will receive the best care and that every doctor and nurse attending him will be blessed and guided. Donna is an electroencephalograph (EEG) tech at the Veterans Hospital in Gainesville. She says Ryder Trauma Center is one of the finest facilities in the world, and that Alan couldn't be in better hands. Still, I can't keep from worrying about his condition. All they will tell us is that he's sustained a serious head injury, and is in critical condition.

When our children were young, if any of them got so much as the sniffles I was on the phone to Doctor Frederic Freidman, our family pediatrician in Miami Beach who still made house calls. Alan suffered from repeated painful ear infections that brought him to tears. Many a time I'd bring him in his pajamas and Bullwinkle slippers to this very kind doctor we referred to as our hero.

Staring out the window of the SUV, I think about Alan's first Halloween. Donna had dressed him in a little bumblebee costume, painted the tip of his nose shiny black and his cheeks rosy red. He was so cute we called him "Bee". That's how he got his nickname.

On a visit to Donna's parents' house in New Orleans, our two-year old Alan pulled off another successful escape. He unlocked the front door and walked two blocks along a canal. A couple who had just happened to be out in their front yard, saw him and realized he wasn't supposed to be there. They lured him over with a red balloon and detained him, anticipating the search party. Sure enough, Donna showed up to claim her little runaway. Later, she told me she had gone out of her mind with worry and was terrified he might have fallen into the water. It was another notch for the guardian angel watching over this child.

Our precocious, lovable, and daring, Alan Michael "Bee" Horton was also an avid collector. At age five, he tugged his little red wagon around our neighborhood and proceeded to remove every concrete water-meter cover on the block.

"Dad, look!" he boasted, smiling proudly as he revealed his loot.

The 20 water-meter covers in his Radio Flyer were 8"x 3" cement disks, not only heavy but hard to remove. Terror-stricken over the number of lawsuits that could be filed against me for broken ankles, I quickly helped my tiny "junk man" cover the gaping holes he'd left in the middle of the sidewalk.

While on vacation in my hometown of Galveston, Texas, I took our children to the Confederate Air Museum. Austin, Anna, and I were looking at a P-51D Mustang when I realized Alan was missing. Turning around, I spotted him in the middle of the hangar. He had just finished unscrewing the last of a dozen floor sockets. He was curious about how things worked and loved taking objects apart and repairing them. He was good at it, too. It was a trait that would serve him well in the future and turn a tidy profit. He once salvaged a broken electric fan, fixed it and sold it for $10.

Always the entrepreneur, he made a bundle in elementary school peddling candy and chips, eventually becoming known as the "Candy Man". I'd been a good horse trader in my day, but Alan never lost money on a deal.

"Dad, I buy a box of 12 bags of potato chips for $1.50 and sell 'em for 50¢ each. That nets me $4.50 in pure profit."

He was persuasive, and even if you saw it coming you'd buy whatever this kid with the irresistible smile was pitching. I had done the same selling fireworks when I was little. Later on, when I was 15, it was hand-drawn hot-rod T-shirts. Alan could have sold an Eskimo ice cubes.

"Dad," he'd say, "someday, when I'm rich, I'm buying you a Ferrari."

"You know, Bee, I believe you will."

Donna and I are coming up on Yeehaw Junction, the halfway point between Miami and Gainesville. Seeing the turnpike exit sign evokes sad memories for me. This was our drop-off and pick-up point for bi-weekly visitations while we were going through our divorce. Donna would drive off, with the kids waving goodbye to me as they left for Gainesville. Driving back to Miami, I'd cry all the way from Yeehaw Junction to Fort Lauderdale.

After our divorce, I became a single dad and raised them for the next six years. Though exhausting at times, it was the most joyful time of my life. Today, we speed by that exit without stopping, without talking.

I think of Alan's phone call from yesterday. He told me he'd stopped a man from beating up a woman in a parking lot. They wrestled, and the guy got Alan in a headlock. Jessie jumped on the guy's back and clawed at him until Alan broke free.

"Dad, I couldn't just stand there. I saw him punch this girl in the stomach."

When Alan was in kindergarten, I had put boxing gloves on him and showed him some moves. I always told him, "Keep your guard up, son, and you'll be able to handle yourself in a tough situation."

A few weeks prior to his accident, while dining at a restaurant in South Beach, another man made a derogatory remark at Jessie. Alan stood up and confronted him.

"Hey! Did you just say something to my girlfriend?"

Though the guy towered over him, Alan stood his ground. The man apologized admitting his remark was just a misunderstanding and invited Alan and Jessie to his table, where they all enjoyed themselves for the rest of the evening. The man was former NBA basketball star Dennis Rodman.

We are finally arriving at the hospital. Suzanne, Bruce's sister, is waiting outside to escort us to the ICU. As we go up, I picture Alan greeting me with a smile, his head wrapped in a bandage as he exclaims, "Wow. Dad, can you believe this? *I* fell." Exiting the elevator, the large double-doors of the ICU ward loom before us. Nothing prepares me for what I am about to encounter. Those doors might just as well have been the gates of hell.

CHAPTER SIX

Walking into the ICU, I scan the beds before me as I search for Alan's smiling face. I'm anxious to see him and give him a big hug. The nurse brings us to our son's bed.

My heart almost stops. Before us is our precious Alan, a bandage around his head and a ventilator tube taped into his mouth. He is unconscious. I reach for one hand as Donna takes his other. His large, calloused hand is warm and has a strong pulse—a good sign. I lean in close as I tell him,

"Hey little Bee, it's your daddy. We're here honey, your mom and I are here."

My words elicit no response. I look at Donna. She covers her mouth with her hand and begins to cry, saying,

"No, no, no, this cannot be happening."

I study Alan's face. He's looking down, appearing as if he's reading a book. The nurse then tells me,

"He's in a coma. He's suffered a severe head trauma as a result of his fall. He also has other serious injuries, a lacerated liver and fractures to his cervical spine."

"How long before he comes out of the coma?" I ask.

"The doctor will explain everything," she replies.

All sense of time is suspended as I feel myself moving into a state of heightened vigilance. The doctor approaches us and begins to describe the extent of Alan's injuries.

"There is almost no brain activity whatsoever," he says, striking terror in my heart. "Your son has sustained a severe injury to his brain stem."

"So operate!" I demand. "You can perform surgery to relieve the pressure on his brain, right? Why isn't that being done? He's alive. He's warm and breathing. For God's sake, do something. Let's get him into surgery, now."

My pleas are fired at him as if I'm unloading a magazine of disbelief and contempt.

"Mr. Horton, at this point, surgery would be superfluous."

"Superfluous? Really? What the hell is superfluous when it comes to saving my son's life?"

I want to knock him down with the hardest punch I can throw. Picking up on my hostile attitude, he turns to Donna and says,

"Maybe you should take a look at his CT scan. I can explain in better detail if you can see what's going on."

A few feet from Alan's bed, we stand in front of a large computer screen that displays the damage done to our son's brain stem. I'm not sure of what I'm looking at, but Donna does. Staring at the images before us, her eyes fill with tears as she begins to shake her head back and forth. I ask her, "What's happening?"

"It's not good, Mike. It's not good at all."

My heart goes over a cliff into a dark abyss of despair. I stare at the doctor and attending nurses. Everything inside me is crying out to them to refute these facts, to change reality, to alter time and space so my son will get well. Only kind, compassionate looks meet my helpless gaze.

Donna speaks first,

"Mike, we might have to take Alan back to Gainesville with us."

"Sure, of course. We can take care of him until he recovers." Lowering her voice, she then tells me,

"Alan may not recover entirely. If he lives, he could be in a vegetative state, possibly for the rest of his life. This is something we have to consider."

I cannot comprehend the thought of Alan being paralyzed for life. I flash back to the time he leapt over a hedge as tall as my chest. He'd cleared it, but it startled me. "That's my power jump, Dad."

"Bee. Please don't do that to me son, you're freakin' me out here, okay?"

"Sorry, Dad." He grinned.

I struggle to grasp the doctor's diagnosis and Donna's comments. I make a phone call to Susie, who's more like my sister than my niece. She was the head nurse of an ICU in Texas. Whenever there is a crisis or a major event, we always call each other for prayers. I'm fighting back tears as I manage to tell her,

"Susie, Alan's had a bad fall. We're in the ICU in Miami. His eyes are fixed and dilated and the doctor is telling me he has irreparable brain damage. Is it possible that Alan can come through this?"

"Do you want me to fly to Miami?" she asks,

"I think it's too early to say," I tell her. "Please start a prayer vigil for Alan. I'll keep you posted with updates." I turn to the nearest nurse. "I need a priest. Now, please. If things take a turn for the worse, I want my son to have the Last Sacraments."

"I believe the priest already came," she replies.

"We just got here." I tell her, "How could that have happened?"

"We saw on his driver's license record that he listed himself as Catholic, so we notified a priest immediately."

I persist.

"Please, would you call him back? I have to be sure." She replies,

"There's a priest on call. I'll get him."

I'm relieved to know Alan still has an attachment to his Catholic faith. Before they were born and even to this day, I pray for each one of my kids. I recite rosaries and 54-day novenas to the Blessed Mother and have masses celebrated on their behalf. I pray to God to deliver them from drugs, car wrecks, bad partner choices, and after they experience the grace of a happy death, that each be blessed with eternal life in Heaven.

Jessie stands nearby and tells me that Alan had taken her to mass several times. Smiling, she recounts,

"There was a lot of standing up and sitting down. Even though I'm not a Catholic, I followed him up to the altar. I didn't want to just stand there with my arms crossed when the priest offered me the host, so I took Holy Communion. Later, when I told Alan how embarrassed I was, he just laughed and said not to worry about it."

Agreeing with Alan, I tell her that I don't think God minds too much.

Jessie trembles as she begins to tell me about Alan's fall.

"I'm sitting in the car waiting for him to finish cleaning a window. He's on top of the ladder calling out to me." 'I'll be finished soon, babe, then we'll head for the beach.' That was the last thing he said. I saw a shadow fall past me. I knew he'd hit the ground. He jumped up after the fall and stood for a moment, but I could see in his eyes that something wasn't right. He collapsed, and I started screaming for help. He was unconscious and I was hysterical. I called 911, and then Armando. I don't understand why it took the paramedics over 30 minutes to get there. They had to airlift him out to Ryder. It was horrible."

I sob and hug Jessie as she recalls the last precious seconds of my son's life. I walk over to Alan and clutch the hand that had thrown me so many hi-flying baseballs in our games of catch. The last time we were together we had our gloves and played for a while.

Jessie is inconsolable and constantly hovers over Alan, murmuring into his ears, and reminding us to keep talking to him in case he can hear. I do a lot of this in the beginning, but now only in intimate prayer and only when Alan and I are alone.

"Window Guy" was the original name of the family business I turned over to Alan when I left Miami in 2006. I never trademarked the name, but a rival company did. So, Alan changed it to "Window Washing Guy" and shrewdly grew the business. It provided the means for him to attend Miami Dade College as a nursing student, and also pursue a career in photography and art.

An African priest from Ghana shows up. I point to Alan and implore him,

"Father, please give my son the Last Rites."

"The Anointing of the Sick has already been administered," he informs me.

"But father, when did you do that?"

"As soon as they took him off of the helicopter. He was anointed with oil and given communion." He then inquires, "Do you or your family need any additional prayers?"

I accept his offer, and thank him as he blesses all of us. Watching him leave the ward floor, I thank God Alan has been given this most important sacrament of all. He has received all of the graces that come from Christ's sacrifice on the cross, and the promise of eternal life with Our Father in Heaven.

CHAPTER SEVEN

Daylight slowly gives way to sunset as the hours melt together, distorting my sense of time. Frequent cups of coffee help me to stay awake through the night.

Sitting beside Alan's bed, I think of what Bruce said to me, before Donna and I left Gainesville.

"Our daughter fell off of our roof one time and she was okay. Don't worry. Alan is going to be just fine."

I hold on to those words. His daughter fell off a one-story house and recovered. Alan fell two stories onto hard concrete.

I take short breaks to call family and friends for advice, prayers, and moral support. Austin, who lives in Los Angeles, will catch the earliest flight available. Anna is working on a ranch in Arizona, and won't be able to fly out until tomorrow morning. I pray both will arrive in time to be here with their little brother, to hug him and to say goodbye.

"I can't believe this." Austin says on the phone. "I'm devastated."

He arrives, walks in, and places his hand on Alan's forehead.

"Bee," he cries. "I'm here, baby brother, I'm here."

Tears pour like rain from all of us. Austin's love for Alan is immense. They grew up together and Austin taught Alan those lessons in life only a big brother can impart. We spend the night taking shifts; several of us keeping watch while others bring coffee from downstairs.

Anna arrives in the morning. I hug her tight as she enters the ward. She is silent as she lightly treads up to Alan's bedside. Carefully, she examines her brother's injuries as if she were looking for clues or significant information to explain his condition. She doesn't speak and she doesn't cry. She gazes at him lovingly and then walks over to me. I put my arm around her as she leans her head against me. We just stand there for a long time. There are no words. We are speechless.

As his older sister, Anna was always watching out for Alan. Once, when they were little, he had dropped his new glasses down a storm drain. Fearing what punishment I might mete out, she took him to a nearby optometrist's shop that advertised free glasses. After being informed she would have to pay $200 for the frames that came *with* the lenses, she begged the puzzled clerk.

"Could I please have the lenses anyway?" she entreated. "I can make frames out of black Playdough."

Dismissed, she returned home to stand beside her panic-stricken little brother. When she told me the whole story, I had to laugh, but I greatly admired her courage and loyalty to her little brother. Returning to the scene of the crime, I held Alan tightly by his ankles and lowered him into the drain for a successful retrieval.

"Beedo, found humor in everything," Anna recollects, "like the quirky Christmas card he drew for Dad that depicted happy people parachuting down on to the deck of the Titanic. He was always putting on little shows, or playing practical jokes, like planting fake cockroaches around the house. There's a photo of him at Disney holding a 'Crush, The Sea Turtle' doll. You can see in his eyes that, at the time, he thought this doll was the cutest thing on the planet. He's always been there for me and never held his love back. He has such a big heart and he's always put his love for others in front of himself. I cherish that the most about him."

It was true. Alan never thought twice about helping anyone. Including me.

I thought of the surprise gift he gave me once for Father's Day. He cleaned, organized, and painted my entire shop for me. It was a monumental task, but he did it for me out of love. On another occasion, I asked him if he'd like to help me replace the shop roof. He jumped into the job with the same joy and gusto he always did with any project he ever undertook. He tarred, papered, and shingled the entire roof—and did it all in half a day.

―――

The staff at Ryder Trauma Center has set up an adjoining conference room to the ICU to accommodate all of our family, and our support team, which includes Bruce, his wife Leilani, and their daughters, Hope, Morgan and Edan; Suzanne, and her son, Jason; the twins, Armando and Enrique, are always present; Donna's sister Patricia, and her sons, Luke and Francis, who drive in from Tampa; and our friend Linda, who supplies an endless stream of provisions. In situations of extreme stress, going out for food is not an option. Neither is sleep.

Donna stays by Alan's side.

When he was a baby, she'd rock him in her arms and sing to the tune of "Rock of Ages": "Rock a baby, doh-dee-doh." Alan would squeal with delight, as she'd swing him high and low. He was the youngest, and as everybody knows, the new baby always gets extra attention.

I smile as I recall when we lived in New Orleans and Anna was the new baby. Walking into our kitchen one morning, I discovered three-year old Austin, feeding his baby sister breakfast cereal.

"Austin, that's so sweet of you to help out with Annie's breakfast. What are you feeding her?"

"Peanut butter and Rice Krispies."

I could tell by Anna's pained expression and pursed mouth that milk was not included.

Within a few hours everyone hears the news about Alan's accident, and a host of his friends begin flooding in and out.

In the hospital hallway, a young woman named Melissa approaches me and tells something that epitomizes the quality of Alan's compassion.

"Are you Alan's father?"

"Yes, I am."

"Years ago, I was in elementary school with your son. Alan was always popular. I was shy and overweight and nobody ever talked to me except him. Alan always remembered my name. He was the only one from grade school who did. I'll never forget him for that. His kindness meant so much to me."

Holding back my tears, I barely manage to thank her as I think, "My God, how many lives did Alan touch?" More than I could count.

CHAPTER EIGHT

I continue my bedside vigil into the early morning hours, fighting fatigue from lack of sleep. I want to be with Alan every moment I can in case he wakes up. He looks as if he could at any second open his big brown eyes and blink awake, happy and relieved to see loved ones beside him. I don't want to miss that moment and I hope against hope it will come.

Gayle calls to say she's just finished teaching her last class in Gainesville.

"I'm flying down right now," she informs me.

I tell her to grab a cab after she lands and to get here as soon as possible. "I'm so glad you're coming." I tell her.

"My place is there by your side," she replies.

We'd been married for only 14 months but she loves my children as if they were her own. Three hours later, she arrives at the hospital. I thought I'd been holding it together pretty well until I see her, but when she hugs me, I begin to lose it.

Gayle is not an emotional, touchy-feely kind of person. With a Ph.D. in philosophy and an I.Q. that's off the charts, her personality might be better defined as a female version of Spock from *Star Trek*. She's logical, analytical, and a self-professed introvert. She has a quirky sense of humor, and refuses to answer the telephone. She doesn't like being around people, yet she loves teaching and is adored by her students. She detests going anywhere in public, but she'll drive to a neighboring state to go shopping with her mother.

I, on the other hand, am an emotive, creative, sensitive type. Being almost polar opposites, we operate in completely different dimensions, but we do have a lot in common, mostly, we take care of each other and our families.

The stress and sorrow associated with Alan's condition finally takes a toll on Austin. His delayed reaction erupts into an angry outburst.

"Why is this happening? I can't believe this is happening!"

He so distraught and upset I have to coax him away from Alan's bedside and into the conference room. I finally get him calmed down as he says,

"He looks like he could sit up any minute, Dad."

"I know Austin, I know."

Austin recalled that when they were growing up together, Alan would fall asleep with his eyes partly open.

"That used to kind of freak me out," Austin said. "I kept thinking, how can anybody go to sleep like that? But I guess Bee could." Jokingly, he added, "Dad, you know that little flat spot on his ear lobe? I told him it was flat like that because when he was a baby, I squeezed his ear so hard it stayed that way forever." We laugh, but only briefly.

Austin has been a great big brother to Alan. He's always been his protector, confidant, guide, and bodyguard. With extreme frustration and guilt now, he tells me, "Somehow, someway, I should have been there to protect Alan from that fall. After all, that's what a big brother's supposed to do."

Austin doesn't realize that had it not been for him watching over his younger brother all those years, Alan might've been hurt or injured dozens of times. I try to reassure Austin that nobody could have been a better big brother to Alan than he was.

My friend Mickey had started a prayer vigil for Alan. He's booked a room in a hotel so I can sleep for a couple of hours. I thank him but think it's best to stay at Alan's bedside. Donna tells me she is not leaving Alan for any reason.

Still, as the hours wear on into the night, I'm so exhausted I start seeing and hearing things that aren't there. I don't know how long I've gone without sleep. Days and nights have blurred together distorting my sense of time and space. After some prompting from Gayle, I decide a nap might re-energize me. We cab across town and attempt to grab a nap, but in the hotel room I can't relax worrying about Alan. As soon as I get under the covers, my cell phone rings. It's the ICU calling to say Alan is in cardiac arrest and we need to return as soon as possible.

I beat myself up as we hurry back in a taxi. I should have never left Alan that window-washing business, I thought. If it weren't for me he'd never have been up on that ladder in the first place.

The cab pulls up and we bolt for the elevator. In the ICU, the heart-monitor alarm screams out a cardiac-arrest warning as a team of doctors and nurses swarm around Alan.

"Bee, don't give up, baby," I shout. "Fight, son. I'm here, we're all here."

The monitor keeps screaming. We stand a few feet away, helpless as our child fades.

"Please save him," I cry out. "Oh, God, please do something."

Alan is not responding. He is crashing. In a final desperate attempt, the doctor slams his fist down on Alan's chest as hard as he can. My reaction is to hit him back for hurting my boy, but suddenly the heart monitor shifts into to a steady pulsating sound. Alan is back. This doctor has just saved our son's life. Yet, Austin crumples to the ground, screaming and crying.

"I felt Alan's soul leave his body." He sobs, "Dad, I was standing right next to him. Bee's gone."

Austin becomes so hysterical, I fear security might intervene. I escort him off the ward floor. Although I understand his anguish, I don't want staff getting involved. Austin is a former wrestler and not someone you'd want to tangle with.

Donna also thinks Alan is gone.

"He is still alive," I insist. "His hand is warm. His cheek is warm. He's in a coma. I will not let my son die."

CHAPTER NINE

Friends of Alan's stream in and out of the visitor's area the remainder of the day, exchanging stories of how he helped them in some way.

Enrique tells me, "Alan was my first true friend. He was my wingman. He never told me he couldn't talk or spend time with me and he'd literally drop whatever he was doing to listen to my joys or my sorrows. He taught me to live life to the fullest."

Armando gives an almost identical account, "The first real friend I ever had was Alan. He was there for me and anybody else who ever reached out to him. Whether we were on the football field, in school, or out partying, he'd always be the guy you'd want to have your back. We were the 'Three Musketeers.'"

Long time family friend, Jason, says of Alan, "He was good at everything he did. He was a gifted entrepreneur and a generous friend. I was late for work one day and was freaking out because my car wouldn't start. Alan pulled up on his new mini-bike, flipped me the keys, and said, 'Here, just take my scooter.' I made it to work on time and saved my job. Alan was only 11 years old but he was more mature than all of us at that time."

Jason and I talk about Alan's film projects. Video photography was another talent of Alan's. I have a dozen DVDs with all of our home movies on them, many depicting Alan's improvisations, comedy skits, and his favorite—stop motion animation. I have all of those on DVD. I have those. Thank God.

The doctor who saved Alan from cardiac arrest approaches me. I begin to thank him when he abruptly tells me, "Look you need to make a decision. Your son is never going to wake up." And I go numb.

"I am the resurrection and the life, saith the Lord he that believeth in me, though he were dead, yet shall he live and whosoever liveth and believeth in me, shall never die." John11-25: 26

Several months before Alan's accident, I felt compelled to call each of my children and ask them if they believed Jesus Christ was their Lord and Savior and died on the cross to redeem their sins.

"Absolutely, for sure!" Austin and Anna replied to my great relief.

"Dad, of course I believe that," Alan assured me.

"Okay, just checking." I told him. "I wouldn't want to get to the end of my life and have God ask me if I'd ever taught my children that Christ died to give them eternal life."

All three guaranteed me I'd done a good job instilling those beliefs in them. Alan informed me that he and Jessie had been "church shopping" recently. I was thankful to know he'd begun his spiritual journey. It was a great consolation to me that Alan was in touch with God.

It's Friday morning. Alan has been taken into organ recovery surgery. Our procession makes it's way back through a maze of corridors to return to the ICU ward. Some of us are silent, most of us are crying.

On arrival, I immediately feel a sense of emptiness. I look at the space that we'd all huddled in for the past five days. It is now empty. The medicine delivery units, the IV racks, all of the equipment used to sustain my son's life has now vanished. No more beeping sound emanating from a ventilator or heart monitor. Sunshine streams in through the windows and across the vacant floor. It is quiet and it is time to go. There is nothing left to hold, to touch, to say.

We collect our things from the conference room as we prepare to leave. I thank the doctors, nurses and staff for valiantly trying to save Alan's life, and I remain grateful for the tenderness and mercy shown by the hospital administration of Ryder Trauma Center and by the representatives of LAORA.

I discuss funeral arrangements with Donna, our children, and Gayle. We all agree we don't want to see Alan displayed lifeless, in a casket. We'd rather everyone remember him as he lived—smiling and squeezing them in a bear hug with his huge muscular arms. Donna will keep his ashes but I implore that she never scatter them. She agrees.

We decide on two memorial services, one in our old neighborhood on Miami Beach, and the other in Gainesville. I suggest that Mickey conduct the Miami memorial service, and we all agree.

In the afternoon, Armando drives us to the home of our friend, Dee Dee, who lives just two doors down from our old house in the neighborhood where Alan had grown up. She insists that we spend the remainder of our stay in Miami Beach with her.

En route, I receive a call from an old Galveston friend who tells me she's had a dream indicating Alan was now in Heaven with my mother and my sister, Rosemary. I recalled John 11; 25-26: "He who believeth in me, though he were dead, yet shall he live: and whoever liveth and believeth in me, shall never die." Though Alan was gone, in her dream my mother and sister were saying, "We've got him now!"

Catholics believe in the Communion of Saints: the souls of the departed who are now in Heaven. (One's family, friends, and ancestors.) I begin to think of Alan, smiling and laughing with my family in some incredible paradise beyond my comprehension, where all is well and no one cries for their child anymore.

CHAPTER TEN

Dee Dee's was an integral part of our lives on Post Avenue. When our children were out and about in the neighborhood, they would hang out there most of the time. It was Alan's favorite watering hole for cookies, milk, lemonade, or whatever Dee Dee had to offer to the pack of munchkins that seemed to revolve endlessly in and out between her kitchen and into her back yard.

During my single parenting years, there were many times I'd pull into the driveway after work and see Dee Dee standing in the front yard with my children and our babysitter. After putting in a full days work herself, and with her own family to raise, she still found time to walk over for a "Dee Dee check" on the Horton family. "So, Michael how was your day?" She'd offer, "I'm going to Publix to get milk, can I bring you anything?" Always with a cheerful smile, she was comforting and supportive to all of us in those days.

Even now, years later, she is stepping up to the plate once again for Alan and for the family she loves, as we try to negotiate our way through numbing grief.

Dee Dee's home is like an oasis after the ICU ward at Ryder. Shaded by a canopy of tropical trees and coconut palms, her back yard will serve as the site for Alan's Miami Beach memorial. It is a fitting place to honor my son; underneath those very branches where he had played as a child.

I walk out to the front of the house and look up and down Post Avenue. The small street is lined with Royal Poinciana trees on either side, the limbs intertwining above to form a tunnel of green. It's exactly what Dee Dee had had in mind when she planted all those saplings 15 years ago.

As a child, Anna was in charge of watering the tiny branch Dee Dee planted in front of our house. Whenever I'd jokingly refer to her rows of saplings as "The Magnificent Post Avenue Dee Dee Memorial Parkway," Dee Dee would grin, shake her finger at me, and say, "You just wait and see Michael Horton. Someday our street will look just like Miami's Coral Gables!" Well, darned if she didn't pull it off.

I remember the whistling sound of Alan's "Vortex Howler," a small football-shaped, rocket torpedo with fins, and sound effects, as he would throw it high into the blue sky above Post Avenue. Alan could easily hurl that thing a city block, and I'd have to scramble to get a fix on it as it soared high overhead like a buzz bomb.

Austin is now carving something into the trunk of the Royal Poinciana in our former front yard. I walk down to join him and to read what he's engraving. *Alan was here.* We hug each other and cry. To this day, Dee Dee's son and Alan's childhood friend, Garman, recarves those words each year to make sure they never fade away.

In the evening, we drive over to collect Alan's things at his high-rise apartment adjacent to Biscayne Bay. Upon entering, I'm gladdened to see he'd provided a gracious home for Jesse and himself. Handsomely decorated with modern furniture and appointments, it was another reflection of his taste for the good things in life.

I'm holding it together fairly well until we walk into the spacious bedroom. In the corner is the painting Bee had been working on. We'd been discussing it together over the past few weeks; he'd ask for my advice on which brushes to use for his fine details and line work. I had mailed him some brushes, and suggested that the sign painter's brush was best for what he was doing. His work-in-progress depicted an array of brilliantly colored geometric shapes. We'd talked about the painting at length, including the gesso primer. I've always freely and lovingly supplied the children with funds for their creative endeavors. Whenever Bee ran low on colors, I'd replenish his paints (especially his favorite: cobalt blue). I felt honored when he sought my help and advice, and it was something he did all his life. A sweet kid, he always thanked me profusely.

Alan's first venture into creating imagery on canvas was impressive. His draftsmanship and execution were flawless, and he'd been so excited about his first serious painting ever. Like everything else he attempted, he threw himself into it 100%. Tears welled up as I reached out to touch the canvas. His painting that he so loved would never be finished.

Sorting through his personal papers, I realize he has saved every card, cartoon, and correspondence I've ever sent to him, including my last letter dated May 30th, 2010. I wrote of how proud I was of his accomplishments and I complimented him on his sensitivity, talents, and his sense of wonder. I told him to nurture his faith and always include God in his plans, and he would be successful.

We cull a myriad of papers, documents, and personal belongings, scanning for any item that will have a shred of significance to a grieving family member. Desperately, we all search through boxes, clothing, and drawers. I find his camera, a new Canon digital that I had promised him I'd go in on 50-50. " Alan, you save half and I'll match it." The memory card is missing. We never find it; nor do we ever find his wallet.

Jessie, having just lost the love of her life, now watches as we descend upon the intimate space she'd shared with Alan. We dismantle and disassemble anything we can carry out in our arms as she looks on in silent dismay. For any undue hurt I may have caused her by my own insensitivity, I pray she will forgive me. I was doubled over with pain and could feel nothing but despair.

I wonder if Alan chose this high-rise because it reminded him of being up on the mesas of the Southwest. When we lived on Post Avenue, I would pile everybody in the van and drive up to the top of the six-story parking garage off Arthur Godfrey Boulevard and Prairie Avenue to watch the sun go down. We'd bring fast food and have a joyous time up there with our own little family on our very own mesa, at the top of the world.

Immediately after he was born, Alan was taken from his mother to a table where silver nitrate drops were put in his eyes. The nurse then picked him up and handed him to me. Though Donna had carried him for nine months, I was the first to hold him…and the last to let him go. Now, as everyone waits in the hallway, I'm the last to leave. I linger in the doorway. It's so hard to let go.

"The Lord is close to the brokenhearted and saves those who are crushed in spirit." Psalm 34:18

Still in shock and visualizing Alan under a white shroud with a rose on it, I am incapable of tending to the logistics of my son's memorial service. I can barely remember my own name.

Sunday arrives. Unable to make the obituary deadline for the newspaper, I worry that Alan's service might go unnoticed. I'd forgotten about the effectiveness of the digital grapevine. Alan's friends, alerted by cell phones, Facebook, and Twitter, come in throngs to Dee Dee's peaceful and serene backyard. I think of little Alan, Garman, and their pals, romping with squirt guns and cowboy hats through this lush tropical scene that had been their childhood playground. It's the perfect place for his friends, schoolmates, and teachers to commemorate him.

Rosie is one of the first to arrive. I'm overwhelmed with emotion as she approaches me. Without words we hug and through her tears she tells me, "I collapsed when my mother told me Alan had been taken off life support. I would've been there for him had I known he was in the hospital. Alan was my 'twin flame': the mirror image of my soul, the one I connected with the most. I feel so badly about not being able to tell him that he was my one true love. I will never meet another man in my life that will treat me like he did or measure up to him. I broke his heart, and it was my own selfish decision. I wish I'd had the chance to re-kindle that flame with him. He had this light about him; he loved bringing people together to have a good time. He wanted everyone to be happy."

Through the heart of this twin flame, I'm granted a glimpse into the depth of the love they shared. Though brief, it burned brightly for them both. It gives me great joy to know that Alan experienced such a love at least once in his life.

Mickey shows up early with his guitar and a folder full of programs he's designed for the memorial service. There's a striking black-and-white photograph of Alan in his grandfather's drayman's cap. He looks as if he could've been a movie star on the set of John Steinbeck's "The Grapes of Wrath." Under the photo are the words:

Alan Michael Horton.
To our son, brother, and friend.
February 24, 1985—October 19, 2010.

The service begins with Mickey leading us in prayer. Austin performs "While You Were Sleeping" by Elvis Perkins. Anna sings the 19th century Gospel hymn "Angel Band." And our friends, Morgan, Hope, and Edan, sing our family favorite, Alison Krauss's "Down to the River to Pray." Although a professional singer all my life, I would crumple to the ground if anyone were to ask me to sing Alan's favorite, "The Lion Sleeps Tonight."

Alan's service is supposed to be a "celebration" of his life, but I'm way too busted up inside to celebrate anything.

Finally, it's my turn to speak. Being Alan's father was like trying to hold on to a shooting star. There had never been a dull moment. I tell of his funny escapades, his love of life, and his courage. I try to provide a mural of his life with a postage-stamp sized image. I do my best. Thinking back, I don't remember much of what I said at all. At the end of the ceremony, I quoted a poem by Kahlil Gibran, "On Children," from *The Prophet*:

> You are the bows from which your children fly
> As living Arrows are sent forth.
> The archer sees the mark upon the path of the infinite. And
> He bends you with His might.
> That His arrows may go swift and far.
> Let your bending in the archer's hand be for gladness; for even as He loves the arrow that flies, So He loves also the bow that is stable.

CHAPTER ELEVEN

Monday morning, Dee Dee is hugging us and trading tearful goodbyes. Bringing the luggage out to our vehicles, my heart skips a beat. Parked in front is Alan's black Nissan truck. The last time I saw it, he and Jessie were leaving our house in Gainesville to return to Miami. Flashing a smile and waving goodbye, he drove away and disappeared around the corner. It was the last time I'd ever see my boy alive.

We wanted Jessie to have Alan's truck. This morning she brought it over for Gayle and I to use as there were too many of us to fit into the SUV that Donna and I drove down in.

Standing in the early morning light, I take a last look down Post Avenue. I'm just about to open the door of Alan's truck, when a car stops beside me. I recognize the driver immediately. It's my old friend, Malcolm. Leaning toward me, his wife Kay asks, "Mike. What a surprise. It's been years since we've seen you and the kids. What are you doing back here in Miami?"

It would be the first of many similar scenarios to come, that of having to inform friends of Alan's death.

When I was a single parent, Malcolm's family and mine would attend Sunday mass together. Their son, Blake, had been a close friend of Alan's when they were Cub Scouts and I was their den leader. One night I called Kay in a panic when Alan had been running a high temperature. She dropped everything and came running over to our house. Luckily she was an RN and assured me that Alan would be fine. She told me she'd always be "right around the corner."

Now I have to tell her that Alan has died. She gasps, clasping her hand over her mouth. Malcolm bows his head. We spend a few moments together and pray before they drive off.

I climb up into Alan's truck. The scent of his cologne, his sunglasses, his carefully maintained logbook, make me feel he was here just minutes ago. I drop the gearshift into low and pull away from the neighborhood we once deemed "our little paradise." Heading across the Julia Tuttle Causeway, I glance back across Biscayne Bay, wondering if I'll ever return to Miami Beach again.

I ask Gayle if she has any quarters for the tollbooth. Once I'm on the turnpike, I completely zone out. The next thing I remember is standing with Gayle in our kitchen in Gainesville.

"What?" she says." You mean to tell me you don't remember we were almost in a wreck?"

"What wreck?"

"It happened on the turnpike, in front of us. A camper top fell off someone's truck. The truck turned over on its side, and the camper continued on in another direction. You were so involved in looking at the camper you almost slammed into the car in front of us. The car that Donna was driving with your own children in it!"

"Why didn't I crash into it?"

"I screamed, *stop!* Then you hit the brakes."

"My God," I exclaim. "We could've all been killed." I'm stunned at having no recollection of this.

Grief trauma is a strange thing. It can suspend time, disrupt event sequences, and distort reality. It may short-circuit the body's tactical response abilities necessary in order to react in an emergency situation. It also greatly affects medium and long-term memory.

According to Elisabeth Kubler-Ross's *On Death and Dying*, grief comes in five stages: anger, denial, deal making, depression, and acceptance.

These stages can appear in any order, in any combination with the other stages, anywhere, anytime, for any reason, and for no reason at all. They can intertwine with one other and morph into something that has no name—something vague and wispy.

Call it the sixth stage of grief. I think of it as "The Fog'" a state of non-awareness or numbness. Psychotherapist Lew Fabrick, Ph.D., diagnoses it as Acute Traumatic Stress Disorder (ATSD), stress occurring within two to three months of a traumatic event. It's different from Post Traumatic Stress Disorder (PTSD), stress occurring after three months and beyond, possibly to the end of life.

At first I think of The Fog as benign—bothersome and inconvenient, and just another phase of grief that will pass. I'm wrong. It descends upon a grieving parent, and it's dangerous. Life-threatening dangerous. I find myself cloaked in a perpetual state of distraction.

CHAPTER TWELVE

Back in Gainesville, I go through the motions of my daily routine on autopilot. I look forward to putting my head down on my pillow this first night back. Sleep is a welcome escape from the thoughts and images streaming non-stop through my mind during my waking hours.

The first chance I get, I make a beeline for one of my support groups at Westminster Presbyterian Church. Trying to maintain my composure, I scan the room and sit down next to James, my African-American friend from Chicago. He'd lost his daughter, mother, and wife all within the last three months.

"Hey, baby, what up?" he says, with a smile.

I look him in the eyes to reply, but break up. All I can get out is, "James I've lost my son." He hugs me and says, "You just sit down right here next to me." He puts his arm around my shoulders and keeps it there throughout the entire meeting.

When it's time for me to share I explain what happened to Alan, and tell them that I called from the ICU ward at Ryder Trauma Center. If it weren't for you guys supporting me at the other end, I'd be going insane. You're the firewall between oblivion and me. God is definitely interceding.

We planned a second memorial for Alan in Gainesville, where he attended East Side High School during the time he lived with his mother. He'd made a lot of friends here. Donna's boyfriend, Ed, was able to secure the Thomas Center, a historical landmark and cultural complex with elegant grounds—the ideal site for a memorial. The date set is Sunday, October 31.

"I believe that I shall see the bounty of the Lord in the land of the living." Psalm 27:13

My mother often used to quote this psalm as I was growing up. I think of those words now as we arrive at the Thomas Centre this crisp autumn morning. I listen to the sounds of birds and water cascading from the large terrace fountain. The sun filters through branches of ancient oak trees, backlighting Spanish moss and bathing everything in a soft golden light. I set up a picture board montage full of photos of Alan. Ed and his friends arrange rows of chairs, an array of computers, and sound equipment.

Over one hundred and fifty people begin to converge on me, taking turns conveying their condolences, all of them well intentioned, but few of them helpful. "It was Alan's time to go." "Nothing happens in God's world by mistake." And the worst, "I know just how you feel—my aunt Margaret lost her pet collie last year and it just devastated her."

I don't mind. Today, words aren't that important to me. People's eyes convey their love and feelings better than words. There's more consolation in a four-second glance than in 15 minutes of "advice" about how I should handle my loss and have "closure." For a parent, who's lost a son or daughter, there is no closure. One of the best things to say to a grieving parent is "I'm so sorry. I don't know what to say."

Leilani Cook, a vocalist and friend of 33 years picks up her hand-held microphone and begins to lead us through an eloquent and poignant service. Bruce reads Psalm 23. "The Lord is my shepherd."

Austin had a recording of Alan's voice on his cell phone and plays it through the sound system. Alan is singing an Irish tune and embellishing it by whistling the melody. Crystal clear, it carries forth across the grounds and out into the surrounding neighborhood. To me, Alan is right here, front and center, singing to us from his heart and soul.

It has been a unique memorial from our musically talented family. Alan, Anna, and Austin have all been singing. The only voice missing is mine, but everyone understands I'm just not up to it.

As the service concludes, it's as if there is one heart, feeling and speaking the same language for all of us.

I'm looking at the sky listening to the last notes of "What A Wonderful World," sung by Louie Armstrong, when the blast of a trumpet introduces "When The Saints Go Marching In." Anna is smiling as she hands me one of the colorful parasols she's decorated for the event. Just like the jazz funerals in Alan's hometown of New Orleans, the trumpet player takes the lead as we all fall into step behind him. Twirling our funeral umbrellas, the procession circles the seating area and exits the terrace grounds as we sing at the top of our lungs, "I want to be, be in that number when the saints go marching in." I'm sure Alan approves.

CHAPTER THIRTEEN

I come from a seashore town in Texas that faces the Gulf of Mexico. Galveston Island was a magical place to grow up. Her greatest attraction was the beachfront that spans the full length of her 26-mile coastline.

I loved beachcombing along the seashore early in the morning at ebb tide, with seagulls calling in the distance and the salt air dousing my senses. I would scour the long rows of seaweed hoping to find any treasure that might have washed ashore in the night. Sometimes, there would be sand dollars, or maybe a Portuguese Man-O-War.

Now my mornings in Gainesville, Florida are radically different. Upon opening my eyes, I'm aware of a new feeling in my heart and soul—a sadness and emptiness I've never felt before. All I can do is to go through the motions. So I take Max, my German Shepherd, on three-mile walks. Sometimes we go twice a day.

I can no longer pray, meditate, or recite my rosary. I don't know what to pray for or to whom. I've always considered myself a good man, though I was pretty wild when I was younger. Still, I managed to get my life together, have a successful career, and begin helping others. I've also felt that I have been truly blessed—until my son fell to his death.

Days turn into weeks, as time seems to creep along. I attend my church meetings regularly and stay connected to my social network. I don't know how to get through this crippling depression without the love and support of these friends. All I can do is cry and I've been crying for three years. My home group has folded itself around me like the wings of a giant angel, protecting me and holding me in a safe cocoon while I ride out the greatest emotional battering of my lifetime.

There's one friend who can always read me from across a football field, especially if I'm too quiet, or don't talk. Sarah is like a sister to me. She simply walks up to me and says, "Come here you." She holds her arms out to me and hugs me tight. I cry into her silently, as my entire body heaves and jerks as if I'm having a seizure. She's done this for three years.

Compassionate Friends was my first foray into an organized grief-counseling group. Its purpose is to support parents who've lost a child. One night I showed up at one of their candle-lighting ceremonies clutching a picture of Alan. I just wanted to tell someone how much I missed him.

We shared our heartaches and losses with each other. I'm thankful for the experiences I had with them and I'm grateful that such an organization exists today.

CHAPTER FOURTEEN

My sister, Rosemary, was my spiritual guidance counselor for most of my life. She was loving, wise, and exuberant. Whenever I'd stop in for a visit she'd squeal with delight and cry out, "Mikie!" She always made me feel special. One of her most memorable quotes was "*im*pression without *ex*pression leads to *de*pression."

I know I've been depressed since losing Alan. I'm also aware that I've been angry. Although I've been attending a lot of church meetings, they don't seem to alleviate the grief that continues to shred my soul to pieces.

I am furious with myself. I wish I knew to call Alan the night before he went to work to warn him. Why couldn't I have been standing at the bottom of that ladder with a giant pillow to break his fall?

God took Alan in the prime of his life. God is to blame for Alan's death, but I can't admit that. Not to God or to anyone else.

Grief has a life of its own, and can be different for each of us. ATSD, which occurs from onset up to three months after the event, and PTSD (which occurs afterward) can leave a person in a precarious state of vulnerability.

I draw these "black cloud and lightning bolt" symbols on my calendar to mark days of extreme stress, sadness, or grief. In practice, my "cloud" keeps lightning bolts stored up and hidden from sight. Then some thought, word, or action will trigger a lightning strike, a bolt that can stun, disable, or end a relationship, job, or even a life.

Part of my vulnerability during my grief over Alan is my hypersensitivity to criticism, or even perceived criticism, of my son. I have this sensitivity to a degree with regard to all my children.

Raising my children as a single father, I developed what I call, the "Mother Condor" complex: Mess with my kids, I dive down and rip your eyes out.

Two weeks after Alan died, my first Mother Condor attack was on Gayle. We're walking our dog one morning when I begin to cry. She gives me a perplexed look and says, "I just don't get this grief thing with you."

"Excuse me? Just what the hell is that supposed to mean?"

I can feel my Mother Condor wings retracting in as I prepare to execute a dead stick dive on this perceived attacker. Her remark strikes me as insensitive and hurtful. Her inability to identify with my emotions infuriates me.

"That's because you've never been a parent. I shouldn't have to explain to you why I'm crying. I'm grieving. That's what people do when they experience a loss. They grieve."

My tirade elicits a Spock-like deadpan from Gayle, which further enrages me. We fall into a smoldering silence. I think to myself, "I can't believe this. First I lose my son. And now I'm going to lose my wife. Because this marriage is over! Obviously, I've made a huge error when I married this rude, callous and uncaring person. I will leave her, and Gainesville as well. I will pack up my van and move back to Texas."

This lightning bolt strikes me square in the most vulnerable part of my heart, the place being used for my grieving process. It is here, that I review past events and fresh hurts associated with the loss of my boy. It is my sacred space, inner sanctum, and fortress of solitude. It needs to be honored and respected by others, and not attacked—especially by my own wife of sixteen months who's gone through this entire experience with me and should know better.

What I don't consider, however, is that my left-brain oriented, introverted, unemotional wife was simply making an observation. As Spock might say, "I do not understand your emotion. It is not logical." Well, of course Spock can't understand emotion; he's half Vulcan. The way Gayle's comment comes across to me is: "Why are you crying? That's stupid. It's been two weeks. You should be done with all of this grieving nonsense, I find it annoying and inconvenient."

I move into the guest room and proceed to isolate in a painful and confused state of mind. I confide in Susie, who says, "Mikie, darlin', I really don't think Gayle would ever maliciously or consciously attack you. It sounds to me like she's having a hard time navigating her way through your grieving process. Gayle is loaded with assets. Do you want a touchy-feely response or some killer lasagna?" Gayle's lasagna is legendary.

We pray together over the phone for peace, faith, and understanding. Though I feel an immense sense of relief, I still haven't completely resolved the issue. So I discuss it with my friend Sarah, who says "Okay, it's like this. You're a dog. She's a cat. You're both different human beings with different make-ups. Gayle sees things matter-of-factly. She recognizes a problem and comes up with a logical solution. She thinks things through. You come from the artist's heart, operating from your senses, feeling things she can't. It's not that either approach is good or bad, it's just the way you guys are. You're both hard-wired differently."

Gayle *thinks;* I *feel*. These character traits of ours have never been tested under fire, until now. We've been married over a year and although we might be aware that our differences exist, it's taken a crisis to bring them to the surface.

CHAPTER FIFTEEN

"Fides Quarrens Intellectum"

(Faith Seeking Understanding)

— St. Anselm of Canterbury, 11th Century

It is faith that eventually conquers grief, but it's a long haul. My search for faith began back in 1975, long before Alan's death, when I was trying to make it as a starving singer-songwriter in Nashville, Tennessee.

My roommate Johnny and I were talking outside of our apartment one day when a bearded guy walks up and informs me, "That medallion you're wearing is an occult symbol. Definitely not cool."

It was a silver ram's head, the astrological sign for Aries, and the symbol for my birthday month of March. My girlfriend had given it to me.

"That was Sam, of Sam the Sham and the Pharoahs," Johnny explains. "They had a big hit called 'Wooly Bully.' Then Sam up and became a Christian minister. He felt he needed to warn you about the thing you're wearing around your neck."

There was a strange feeling in my gut all evening. Later that night, I threw the jewelry piece into the forest.

A month later, Johnny tells me our mutual friend Dave, has scheduled a séance at his home. It sounds like fun to me, but when I suggest we attend, Johnny, the son of a Mississippi Methodist minister, objects.

"Why on earth would you want to go to a séance?"

"I'm searching for confirmation of God's existence, if you really want to know. Maybe I'll get to communicate with an angel or something."

"Mikie, you're never going to meet any angels at a séance. It's dangerous to mess around with the occult."

"Okay, I'll stay home already." I reluctantly concede.

Soon reports of the party that had taken place at Dave's house begin to surface. The participants had indeed made contact with a spirit, and at first they found it amusing. This so-called "entity" revealed facts no mere mortal could possibly know about everyone in the room. However, after an hour, the entity became malevolent and sarcastic. It started disclosing shameful and embarrassing truths about the participants, who, by the way, were all beginning to freak out. Dave stopped the séance, allowing the shaken party revelers to disperse. Within a week, everyone who'd attended were displaying signs of deep psychological disturbances, ranging from nightmares to relationship problems. One of the couples broke up.

A week later Dave's wife calls Johnny in tears. She sputters over the phone, "Dave woke me up in the middle of the night screaming, 'There's something in the hallway by the baby's room!' I sensed a heaviness in the air, something oppressive. Dave grabbed his pistol and yelled, 'I cast you out in the name of Jesus Christ. I cast you out in the name of Jesus Christ!' He pointed his gun in the direction of the hallway and repeated the command 'I cast you out in the name of Jesus Christ!' I was terrified. Then it was like the air broke, like a heavy weight had been lifted up, out, and away. Then every dog in the neighborhood started barking."

Shortly after, Dave and his wife decide to get out of town and take a weekend trip.

"How about house-sitting for us John? Our dog is about to have pups."

"Sure, Mikie and I will be glad to."

Johnny takes the downstairs couch, which puts me upstairs, near the baby's room.

It's Easter weekend, and we have our Bibles to read. Nashville is abounding in beautiful white dogwood blossoms. Legend has it that the dogwood, once as mighty as the oak, was used to form the cross that Christ was crucified upon. This so distressed the dogwood that Christ deemed the tree would never again grow large enough to be used for such a purpose. That night Johnny and I sit in the living room quietly reading our Bibles. I finally get sleepy and go upstairs to the bedroom that had been the site of Dave's spiritual showdown. Whatever Dave did, it worked. The entire house is quiet and calm throughout the night. I sleep like a rock and wake up the next day to a glorious Easter sunrise.

This is my first lesson in the power of faith.

As a musician who loves writing and reggae music and as a God-fearing man who seeks to strengthen his faith, the Rastafarian way of life seemed to be the answer to my prayers. Smoking Blue Mountain ganja—one of the most powerful strains of marijuana—is also part of this religion, and it will bring me closer to God, amen and *aye mon*.

I'm 27 and living in New Orleans when my girlfriend, introduces me to her friend, Richard. Also a musician, he's heavy into the dark arts and satanic worship, but since he has a cool British accent, and knows Robert Palmer, a real rock star, that makes him an okay guy with me. He tells me, "You're really good at that reggae music thing. You should come with me to the Bahamas this weekend and meet Robert. He'd really love your stuff."

I'm enchanted with the prospect, as Palmer's song, "Sneakin' Sally Through The Alley," had been a big hit in the U.S. I accept Richard's offer.

During the flight en route to Nassau, something shifts in Richard. He completely loses it, cursing at me and accusing me of being everything from a CIA operative to a satanic agent. Annoyed, I get up and move to another seat. From the time we land, through customs, and all the way out to the curb where Palmer's black limousine was waiting, he continues his rant. Approaching Palmer, it's clear he's already gotten an earful from Richard. Palmer turns to me as I introduce myself, and with a puzzled look asks, "And you are…?"

Shaking his hand, I reply, "My name's Michael Horton. Richard invited me to come down and be a part of your Magic Christian Band." Palmer was even more baffled.

"I'm sorry, my what? I'm confused here."

"Ha, you're not the only one. Look, it appears that Richard here is having a melt-down and wants me to take a hike."

"Don't listen to him he's a devil," Richard screams. This is my cue to leave.

"Can we drop you somewhere?" Palmer asks.

"Thank you," I said, "I'll catch a cab and be on my way."

Tomorrow, I'll fly to Kingston and check out the reggae music scene. Tonight, I check into a hotel. Thinking over the day's events, I have this disturbing feeling that Richard is the personification of evil.

CHAPTER SIXTEEN

On my flight continuing to Jamaica, I recognize a popular reggae group and strike up a conversation with them. I make friends with Tabby and the We the People Band, and they invite me to join them at Joe Gibbs Recording Studio in Kingston.

As I stare out the window at the blue Caribbean Sea below, I write a reggae song, "The Battle of Orion," about the love between my mother and father. They'd met and married after only three days and loved each other passionately the entire course of their 40-year marriage.

The song was also a battle in the constellation of Orion between my father and an adversary who was trying to kill him. My father won the battle.

After landing, I check in to Mr. Bell's Guest House and settle in among the coconut, mango, and breadfruit trees. After making plans to meet my friends at Joe Gibbs Recording Studio tomorrow, I wander about the neighborhood on foot, as it appears to be safe to travel in even at night.

Morning comes. I have a dip in the swimming pool and a café au lait. I then grab my guitar and set out for Joe Gibbs Recording Studio. My dad had given me the guitar as a present for my fifteenth birthday—a 1965 pre-CBS Fender Stratocaster. It's in mint condition and worth a small fortune.

I wander through streets with names like "Quickstep," "Lady Musgrave," and "New Hope Road." After an hour of walking I realize I'm lost. I happen upon the U.S. Embassy and go in to get help. While I'm asking a clerk for directions, a Jamaican who'd been talking to the Marine guard on duty offers to help me find the studio. His name is Donnie. I figure he's trustworthy because he seems to be buddies with the Marine. We leave the embassy compound and begin walking down Belmont Road.

Donnie asks me if I've ever smoked ganja. I tell him I haven't yet but I intend to try it.

"I've got a stash hidden at my mother's house," he says. "It's on the way to the studio just up ahead on the next street."

Walking north on Belmont Road I see a man leaning up against a telephone pole. As we pass him, I notice that he follows Donnie with his eyes. They nod to each other, which strikes me as suspicious, as if he were on the lookout. I figure he's probably in cahoots with Donnie in the ganja drug trade and is keeping an eye out for the police. I dismiss it and continue to follow Donnie, looking forward to my ganja religious experience.

His mother's house is a nice dwelling in a middle-to-upper-class neighborhood. He motions for me to follow him around the side to the backyard, turning at one point with his finger to his lips as he whispers, "Shhhh. Be very quiet. I don't want to wake up my mother. She's sleeping."

I nod in acknowledgement and continue to follow him around to the back of the house. I'm so distracted by my anticipation of my upcoming religious experience, that I think nothing of his next request.

"Aye, mon, just set your guitar case down over there by the fence, and we'll tiptoe in through the back door."

For a split second, I think, "Hmm, that's an odd request. Oh, I know, he's probably worried I'll bump the guitar case up against the wall and wake up his mom. I know what that's like because moms definitely do not like having their naps interrupted." Incredible as it seems to me in retrospect, I left the most valuable and prized possession of my life, outside in the backyard of a strange house in a third world country.

Donnie opens the back door and smiles as he says, "Okay mon, now we smoke the herb." He motions for me to go in first, reminding me to keep quiet as he raises his index finger to his lips and whispers, "Shhhh."

I walk into a small room with one window, actually a large concrete vent designed to prevent entry yet still provide ventilation. I assume this is a laundry or utility room that's joined to the rest of the house by a kitchen door. Except there is no other door, only the one we just came through which is now being slammed behind me.

Startled, I turn around to see Donnie standing in front of the door facing me. The kind and helpful stranger who only minutes before had offered to introduce me to a new and meaningful religious experience, was now holding a ratchet knife. Putting it to my throat he tells me, "Okay, give me everything you got. Then I'm going to kill you."

He then makes a couple of quick swipes across my throat with his blade to show me he means business. I can't tell if I've been cut or not, but I *do* know it'll be only seconds before I go into shock, and if I don't move, I'm going to freeze, and if I freeze, I'm going to die.

Time has stopped, compressing somehow, as everything shifts into slow motion. I raise my hands and assume the hold-up position as Donnie begins to go through the pockets of my cargo pants. As I begin to pray, my entire life plays out before me. It doesn't flash by, or is it like a fast-forward version of a movie. It's just here. Everything is here all at once.

Every face, event, movie, and conversation, is here: Every sight, sound, song, smell, person, place, or thing. Every joy and sorrow, along with all of the laughter and tears of my entire life, right up to this very second. Every good deed and every bad deed I've ever done. There is no feeling of being judged. It's okay for me to die.

I'm experiencing what is now known as The Life Review. It is a phenomenon that is common to those who have had a near-death experience (NDE). There are no feelings of guilt, shame, or remorse. On the contrary, I feel as if I'm in the presence of some infinitesimal love.

This love surrounds me like a cloak of warmth, like being bathed in a golden light, like being in the presence of God.

Donnie is emptying out the last of my pockets. My time is running out. I wonder if I'll fight or freeze. I remember my father's admonition when I was a kid. I was wrestling with my friend Jim in the front yard when he got the upper hand and was holding me down.

"Don't you ever let a man pin you down."

Donnie finishes cleaning out my pockets. Straightening up, he looks at the small crucifix I'm wearing around my neck and says, "Okay, now give me the cross."

I try to undo the tiny clasp on the chain, but my fingers refuse to obey my brain. I look at him and say, "My hands are shaking so much. Can you undo the clasp?"

As he tries to get the clasp loose, I notice he switched hands with the knife. He's now holding it loosely in his left hand between his thumb and index finger. I know exactly what I have to do, and rehearse the entire sequence in my mind.

I have to get possession of his weapon. At first, I think I'll just try to get the knife away from him and throw it through the window. Then I remember the suspicious looking guy by the telephone pole.

It's possible he might be an accomplice and could be right outside waiting for him. Not a good move.

I'll have to grab the knife by the blade itself because he's holding it by the hilt, eliminating any chance of a handle grab. In the same movement, I'll have to inflict some kind of shock wound. This would at least give me time to figure out what to do next. And I still have time. Although the clock is ticking down, I don't panic. It seems as if I have all the time in the world.

I calculate the path of the knife blade and where I'd have to strike first. I determine that my hand will sustain a wound as a result of grabbing the knife blade as I pull it up, out and away from his grip. I doubt this man simply intends to make me count to a hundred as he strolls off with my guitar. He's going to kill me.

Total elapsed time from the moment he said he was going to kill me, up until now as he attempts to remove my crucifix, has been approximately 15 seconds. I guess that's what happens to time and space when somebody tells you that within a few minutes you're going to be dead. You tend to use your time wisely. I tell myself "Yeah, it's okay to die. It's also okay to live. So, I think if I'm going die today, I'm taking this homeboy with me."

It's been no more than two or three seconds since he's changed knife hands and at any moment this guy is going to be done, and then I'm going to be stabbed to death. My time is up. I take a slow deep breath as I imagine hearing Daddy's voice yell, "Now!"

In one quick move I grab the blade and sweep up and across. With my other hand I grasp the front of his shirt. I'll never forget his face as he stares in disbelief at what is happening. I slash, punch, and kick my way out of that 8'x10' death trap, wrestling with him as we crash through the door and out into the backyard. We're both covered with blood. He screams for me to release the grip I have on his shirt. I scream back: "First you give me back everything you took from me and give me back my father's watch."

Fumbling through his pockets and violently shaking, he returns my belongings. The last thing he gives back is my watch, which hadn't belonged to Dad, and I don't even know why I said that to him; it just came out. I look at the hands, maybe to mark this event in my life. Whatever the reason, I'll never forget the time. It's three o'clock in the afternoon.

Finally I let go of Donnie. He turns and runs off in the direction of Belmont Road. I walk back over to where I'd left my guitar and throw the ratchet knife over the fence at a spot where I knew it can easily be found again as I intend to go directly to the police. Although the blood all over my shirt is not mine, I'm sure I look like I've been in a serious accident. Still, I'm able to flag down a kind Samaritan who drives me to Crossroads Police Station.

After filing a report, we return to the house on Belmont Road. The police quickly find the knife and take photos of the crime scene. The back door is hanging sideways on one hinge and blood is splattered everywhere. It's obvious a violent struggle has taken place here.

The detectives complete their investigation and then drive me to Kingston Public Hospital to treat my hand. I'd forgotten about the deep cut I sustained when I grabbed the blade of Donnie's ratchet knife. It's not causing any pain. I just need a couple of butterflies to close up the wound.

Kingston Public Hospital on a Saturday night is like walking into a bizarre Fellini movie. A young boy with an ice pick still embedded in his back casually strolls past me as an old man paces back and forth, hysterically screaming something in Creole. I ask Thomas, the police guard assigned to escort me, what all the yelling is about.

"Bad Voodoo," he replies.

I'm waiting in the hall with Thomas, when an entourage of uniformed military personnel appear and begin walking toward me. Suddenly I'm gripped with fear thinking that I might be in some kind of trouble.

A man with a chest full of battle ribbons and medals approaches me and introduces himself as the commanding officer of the (JDF) Jamaican Defense Forces. He puts my mind at ease when he tells me he just wants me to "identify someone."

We walk down a long hallway and then enter a room that serves as an alternate ER. Judging by the number of black rubber-sheeted corpses, I gather it's either the anatomy lab or some type of temporary morgue.

The commander walks up to one of three covered bodies and flipping the sheet back on the first, asks, "Is this the man you had the fight with?"

"No, sir."

He walks over to the second table and prepares to uncover another body. As I walk behind him, I look down and to my left. Protruding from underneath the rubber sheet was the floral patterned-sleeve of Donnie's shirt.

"Oh, my God, this is the guy." I point to the covered body in front of me.

The commander approaches the corpse and pulls the sheet back. It's Donnie.

"Is this the man who tried to kill you?"

I reply, "Yes, that's the man."

The commander takes my hand and shakes it vigorously. "Congratulations! I hope you kill every one of these bloodclots."

Stunned, I just stand with a perplexed look on my face.

The commander continues, "Last night a man was killed at Tivoli Gardens over a couple of cigarettes. This man fits the description of the attacker who fled police. We found him dead this afternoon on Belmont Road. He had bled to death. This man was going to kill you."

Taking Thomas aside, the commander speaks to him in Creole. I stand in silence as tears stream down my face. I never wanted to kill anyone. I did this in self-defense. I know that intellectually, but the horrific guilt and memory of his death will haunt me for the rest of my life. I've had masses offered for him. I've confessed this to priests at least a hundred times. It doesn't matter. I just can't seem to forgive myself. And I can still see his face to this very day.

Thomas remarks in his thick Jamaican accent, "Aye, mon, why you crying? You are a hero now. That mon was going to kill you!"

"Look, if I'm free to go, can somebody please just drive me back to my guesthouse? I want out of this place."

"Aye, mon," Thomas says, "But first you need to get you're your hand stitched up."

An attractive young Jamaican nurse renders first aid and tells me in a couple of hours, my hand is going to start throbbing.

"Can you give me something for pain?" She winks at me and says, "I'll be right back."

Thinking she's going to give me something like aspirin, I'm surprised when she hands me two vials of Demerol and a syringe. Slipping them to me under the table, she whispers, "Quick, put these down your pants. Take one tonight and the other tomorrow. Take care of yourself now."

Tonight the Demerol helps me to forget the horror of the day. Blessed sleep comes as I drift off into a deep and dreamless state.

The next morning I'm standing outside by the pool having a cup of coffee when two men in a black unmarked vehicle with U.S. Government plates pull up in front of Mr. Bell's Guest House. They are agents from the U.S. Embassy. Crossroads police informed the embassy that an American citizen had been involved in an altercation and subsequently forwarded my information on to the embassy office. The same office I had visited less than 24 hours ago when I was asking for directions to Joe Gibbs Recording Studio.

The field agent informing me of this, requests that I return to the embassy for a brief meeting with the U.S. ambassador. I oblige, hop into the back seat, and within 15 minutes I'm meeting with the U.S. ambassador to Jamaica. His name, quite coincidentally, is Jimmy Carter.

Ambassador Carter says cordially, "I just want to give you a heads up to be on your best behavior, you're now an American tourist who's in the public spotlight. Here's a copy of the *Daily Gleaner* that's reported the incident in detail.

We shake hands as he delivers these parting words; "You're somewhat of a hero to the locals here. So please don't do anything that would reflect poorly on your new image. In other words, don't get arrested for partaking in any of the local products that are always being hawked to tourists here in Jamaica." I assure him that I'll be careful not to jeopardize my standing in the community.

Walking out of his office, I pass the Marine guard posted by the elevator. I think about the day before, when I'd observed him engaged in friendly conversation with Donnie, and recalled the old saying, "You can't judge a book by the cover."

I finally make it to Joe Gibbs Recording Studio and I explain how important it is that I present my music to them as I'd nearly been killed trying to get here. I take the *Daily Gleaner* clipping out of my wallet and give it to the sound engineer, who in turn shows it to Gibbs himself. He tells me to proceed directly to the studio.

I plug in my guitar, put on headphones, and wait while a drummer and bass player set up to accompany me. On the engineers cue, I begin playing one of my reggae compositions. When I finish, one of the Jamaican musicians asks me, "Hey, mon, how you learn to play reggae like dot?"

"I don't know," I reply, "I've just always done it. It's kind of like surf music, you know, like playing 'Pipeline'."

The sound engineer then says, "Okay, we're going to record you."

They tell me they'll contact me to set up a recording session, and I thank them for their time. I never do reconnect with Tabby or the We the People Band, the musicians who'd invited me to join them here in the first place.

Neville, the drummer who jammed with me, offers to drive me back to Mr. Bell's. On the way, we stop by the house on Belmont Road so I can take photographs of the site. I don't want to forget what happened here. Ever.

I return to Mr. Bell's Guest House and phone my mother in Galveston, since I've been out of touch for days. Halfway through the first ring, she answers, "Michael?"

Trying to keep my composure, I reply, "Hi, mom, I just want to—"

She cuts me off. "Thank God, you're alive. I've been worried out of my mind. Where are you?"

"I'm in Kingston, Jamaica, I came here to—"

She says, "Yesterday, I woke up at three o'clock in the afternoon from a terrifying nightmare. I dreamt a giant black cloud in the shape of an evil looking bird was descending on you. I sensed your life was in danger, so I called everyone in the prayer group and asked them to pray for you."

I am stunned at the synchronicity.

"Mom, at three o'clock yesterday, a man was going to kill me for my guitar. I fought him off, but he died as a result of his wounds. It was self-defense."

She emits a deep sigh before saying, "I knew it. I knew you were in trouble. Praise God for sparing your life."

The Rastafarian lifestyle had been alluring to me. Smoking ganja while playing reggae music was a dream I pursued until it almost cost me my life—all in the interest of increasing my spiritual awareness.

Moral: There is no path to God through drugs.

CHAPTER SEVENTEEN

After losing Alan, I head into the dreaded "firsts": his first birthday date, the first Christmas without him, the first Father's Day without a card or a cheerful call from my youngest son.

Just days after Alan's memorial service in Gainesville, I receive a troubled call from Anna. After returning to her job in Arizona, she soon ends her two-year relationship with her fiancé and co-worker. His inability to empathize with her grief makes it clear he isn't the one for her. She had needed the love and support of a caring partner. Crushed, she finds she must leave her job and her relationship. She is crying and deeply in shock from losing her brother. They'd been inseparable.

"Annie, we're booking a flight home for you," I instruct her, "Pack up everything you own and get ready to leave. Gayle and I want you to come back home and live with us. My cousin Bonnie, who lives in Tucson, is on her way to pick you up and will be there in two hours."

Anna is with us for all of the firsts, and the first hurdle is Halloween, one of Alan's favorite holidays. Handing out candy to little costumed trick-or-treaters I have to hide my tears. I keep imagining I'll see my Bee show up, as a toddler in his little bumblebee costume.

At Thanksgiving, both Anna and I are numb. Only Gayle is operating at a normal level of awareness and proficiency. I ruin the turkey and have to scramble Thanksgiving morning to pick up another one. Dinner turns out fine, thanks to Gayle and Anna, but I find it virtually impossible to muster even a faked shred of gratitude.

Christmas is another walk in the Twilight Zone. I float through the days in a dream-like state, unaware of anything going on around me. I avoid any situation that might remind me of Christmases past, like watching children visit Santa Claus, or worse yet, allowing myself to stumble within range of any Christmas carol wafting through the air. Even my favorite annual viewing of "It's a Wonderful Life" is off-limits.

I almost get through the whole ordeal, except for one night when I accompany Gayle to Toys R Us. I pass by a display rack holding small toy cars—like the ones Alan used to play with. He must've had hundreds. I was always stepping on them and screaming out "Alan! Get in here *this second* and pick these up *right now* or I swear I'm gonna throw all of 'em in the trash. I mean it too, mister Bee." I never did, of course.

When I see these little cars tonight in Toys 'R Us, I just lose it.

If not for Gayle, we wouldn't have had Christmas in our home the first year. Normally, I'm hands-on with any project around the house, but this holiday season all I can manage to do is buy a tree and stick it up. Gayle decorates it, purchases and wraps all the gifts for Anna, Austin, herself, and me, and prepares a delicious dinner.

"Anna and Austin deserve to have a nice Christmas and I'm going to make sure that they get it," she proclaims. True to her word, she pulls it off.

I can't ignore the fact that these events are devoid of their usual celebratory spirit, but I'm thankful Gayle and Anna are here to help me through them—one holiday at a time.

My friend, Frances, arranges a memorial mass to be offered in Alan's honor. Gayle reluctantly agrees to attend despite the fact the Catholic Church abandoned her family at their darkest hour. For Gayle even to walk into a Catholic Church is a rare event.

Her biological father had abandoned them in Scotland in the mid 1970's when Gayle was young, and left his entire family with nothing. After remarrying, the Church excommunicated her mother, an order rescinded with an apology years later—too late to help Gayle, whose Catholic education had long been terminated.

Today, we share intimately with the priest about Alan's death hoping his sermon will reflect our belief that he's in Heaven now, among the angels.

Instead, the priest begins his homily with a hideous rant:

"I know that many of you who've lost loved ones believe they are now somewhere up in Heaven looking down on us from above. Well, they're *not*. They are in *purgatory*!"

We are stunned and in disbelief. With one blow, he shreds my belief and confidence in the Catholic Church. My hope that Alan is safe with God in Heaven collapses. I look in shock at Gayle. Furious, she says, "This is bullshit. Do you want to leave?"

Austin, Anna, and Donna register confusion. I am unable to comprehend this priest's lack of sensitivity and disregard for the emotional state of our family. Not to mention his espousal of an archaic and obsolete myth no longer upheld by the Catholic Church.

At the end of the service, all I can hear is the sound of blood rushing through my temples. Gayle refuses to shake hands with the priest and gives him a look that would scare a ghost. He's not fazed in the least. I shake his hand, typical brainwashed Catholic that I am, but I walk away thinking I may never set foot in a Catholic Church again.

I fall into a depression, which turns into despair. No longer sure of anything I've ever been taught by the Catholic Church, and uncertain of the existence of God and Heaven, I stand at the edge of a bottomless pit.

Alan's decision to be an organ donor saved the lives of three other people. This was our "Bee." Practicing love, faith, hope and charity, up to the very last second of his life. At the time, I thought of his generous donations as being the last beautiful gift he would ever leave behind. I'm so glad I'm dead wrong on this one.

After the purgatory priest, I endure the most horrible year of my life. Thanks to my daughter Anna, January 2011 marks the beginning of an upturn. We take a road trip to Tuscaloosa, Alabama, to see one of her favorite bands. It's a welcome break from the tedium of look-a-like grey days that seem endless. Anna's infectious laughter easily lifts me up and away from my sadness.

At the Old Crow Medicine Show concert, I watch people dancing in the aisles and enjoying life, but at one point I want to jump on stage and yell, "Why are you people so happy? Don't you know what happened to Alan?"

On returning to Gainesville I go to the purgatory priest's church and inform the pastor that the priest's sermon has alienated at least five Catholics who once attended there. Instead of an apology, the pastor defends the priest telling me, "It's unfortunate that happened, but it's probably just a cultural thing. His remarks were more likely the result of the environment he grew up in."

That's it? That's the take on this guy wiping out my faith in the entire Catholic Church? I decide to confront the purgatory priest himself. Cornering him after an Ash Wednesday service, I explain my confusion, disillusionment, and pain. According to Catholic doctrine as I understand it, purgatory is a purification process, not a place. Purgatory is something I'm in now. Alan is beyond it.

I wait in vain for an apology that might wipe away my tears and restore my faith. Mustering a deep breath, he says, "Well, you still have to pay for your sins."

What seminary unleashed this turkey to run wild in God's kingdom, spreading error and disdain across the spiritual countryside like animal droppings? What a heap of dung.

I'm still unresolved about the exact whereabouts of Alan's soul, but as I get up to leave I do manage to say, "You know what? I'll pray for you."

For me, Christ's ultimate sacrifice of dying on the cross, and the shedding of His precious blood for all of us is sufficient for the forgiveness and redemption of sin. Period.

By the same token, I forgive the purgatory priest. I also forgive every priest, nun, and lay teacher along with the Catholic Church for perpetrating antiquated doctrines throughout the course of my Catholic life. They are only human and they too, are sinners, just like me.

Though I do try to pray for this priest and to forgive him, the damage is done. My faith in shreds, I'm spinning into a suicidal depression.

One morning, on a stretch of open road right past Santa Fe College, the speedometer on my Harley Sportster registers 90 mph. Up ahead is an 18-wheeler coming in the opposite direction. For five seconds, I think of aiming my bike at the front grill of the Mack. At this speed I'd feel nothing more than a pin prick—then I'd be in Heaven with Alan. But wait, right now, I don't believe in Heaven. I think of Annie, Austin, and Gayle. I think about the truck driver and his family. I've come to the edge and I'm ready to jump off, but I stop. The Mack blows by me doing at least 50. My "un-belief" just saved me.

CHAPTER EIGHTEEN

Wednesday morning, on the week of Alan's anniversary, I've schedule a 9:30 mass for him at Holy Faith Catholic Church. My pastor, Father John, has agreed to hear my confession following the service.

Walking toward the main building, I stop on the sidewalk where I've had a memorial brick installed with Alan's name and dates on it, along with the inscription: "We love you." It's in front of a statue of Our Blessed Mother, the Jewish mother I entrusted the souls to of all my children at birth. I like to think of Bee as safe in Mary's arms.

I've struggled with so many issues since Alan's death, that I feel a thorough soul cleansing is long over-due. Father John puts me at ease. I disclose my anger and resentments, realizing how much bitterness I still harbor toward the purgatory priest.

Father John relates, "Man, it sounds to me like you're taking poison and hoping the other guy is going to die."

He's right. After leaving his office I feel like I've had a ton lifted off of my chest.

Well into Thursday, I continue to feel uplifted. I hesitate to say "happy", because for a grieving parent, happy is taboo. Sometimes, I wonder if I'm being disloyal to Alan if I haven't spent every waking hour crying or feeling sad. It's a natural part of grief for one who's lost a child.

Friday, October 21st is the day a year ago, that Alan suffered cardiac arrest, and Austin said he felt Alan's soul depart. Gayle and I are discussing a recent visit Anna made to a battlefield in Gettysburg, where over 50,000 Union and Confederate soldiers lost their lives. Pictures that she had taken revealed many strange lights, or "orbs." Gayle inquires, "Hey, didn't you see strange lights when you went on that religious pilgrimage to Medjugorje, Yugoslavia?"

"Yes, I did." I reply, "That's where local visionaries have reported seeing apparitions of the Blessed Mother since 1982. Hundreds of thousands have been traveling there since for physical and spiritual healing—much like Lourdes and Fatima."

Gayle's question surprises me. She's well versed in theology and scripture and spiritual in her own way, but when it comes to anything supernatural or religious, she could care less. I explain to her that I saw the sun appear to spin in the sky. Also, about how I saw a brilliant purple-colored star, emanating rays from a nearby mountaintop. I'd say those were 'strange lights,' so what?

"So, what did you come away with from that experience?" Still stumped by her curiosity, I continue, "I came back with a desire to pray the rosary again with my family which was a tradition I'd learned as a young boy. I also felt compelled to locate the statue of the Blessed Mother that we had when I was growing up. We would always recite the rosary in front of it during the month of May."

This particular statue of Mary had blonde hair and blue eyes. I did an exhaustive search for months, praying to St. Anthony, the patron saint of the lost and found; and to St. Jude, the patron saint of the impossible, but to no avail. I gave up eventually, concluding the statue was most likely lost or broken.

A year after that search, as I'm walking through our neighborhood, I spot a pile of junk near the sidewalk. My friend, Debbie, who is approaching from the opposite direction, sees it too and says, "Oh, look. Cool junk—my favorite thing." On closer examination we realize the items are of great value. Debbie was holding a little figurine of a Cuban man with a burrow, when I saw a wicker basket resting on top of the pile. Out of curiosity I flip it open. In astonishment, I behold a statue of the Virgin Mary; the exact size, height, and color as the one I'd prayed to as a child. The woman who had thrown it out was now staring at me from her front door. "Ma'am," I said, "Is it okay if I take this? Would you like to keep it?" I offered.

She'd obviously been drinking, slurring her words as she replied, "Oh, yeah, my mother just died, but she prayed them rosary beads all her life. She was a Methodist, but she liked Mary. That statue belonged to her, but you can take it along with all the rest of that junk for all I care."

"That's an incredible story." Gayle says, "So, where's that statue now?"

I shrug my shoulders. "I guess it's still in one of the storage bins out in the garage. Why?"

"Go get it."

"Now? Gayle, it's ten o'clock at night and there are eight big storage bins out there. The statue could be in any one of them. Besides, I haven't looked in them for years."

She persists.

"You need to get that statue. I don't know why, but I think you need to find it tonight."

I relent, "Okay, if you feel that strongly about it I'll go look, but I really don't want to start a big project this late at night."

In the garage, I clear away items blocking the first storage bin and open the lid. I see a familiar Quaker Oats box marked "Blessed Mother statue," right before me. I call out to Gayle, "Hey, I found it right here in the first place I looked! How lucky is that?" Walking back into the house, I wonder, "Maybe, this being the one year anniversary of losing Alan, we're supposed to bring the Blessed Mother back into our lives."

I place the statue of Mary on the fireplace mantle next to Alan's picture and light a candle. Gayle and I pray that Alan is at peace and with the Blessed Mother in Heaven.

After wiping away my tears, I pick up the oatmeal box and head back to the garage.

"So, what else do you have in that storage bin?" Gayle asks with a mischievous smile.

I try to plead fatigue.

"Look, honey, it's late. Tomorrow we'll go through all of this stuff together, okay?"

"Well, couldn't you just look in the one you already opened?"

Sheesh, I think. "What is it about my wife and her obsession with these storage bins?"

I turn away from her and sigh with guilt. After all, had it not been for Gayle, I never would've thought to hunt down this precious family treasure—and on this day, of all days.

I lift the lid just high enough to toss the oatmeal box back in when I glimpse the corner of a shiny red piece of paper sticking out from beneath some clothing. Pulling it out, I realize it's a Christmas card—from my Alan. It read:

> "DAD—While looking for just the right present,
> I suddenly knew what to do!
> I took what you've given me over the years…
> [Open up to pop-up Teddy bear art inside of card]
> And I'm giving that LOVE back to YOU!
> *Merry Christmas, Dad,*
> *I love you and wish you happiness and joy this New Year.*
> XXXOOOXXX
> *Love, Alan"*
> *P.S. Happy New Year!*

I look at my wife and explode into tears. Gayle, who never cries, has tears in her eyes as she exclaims, "Oh, my God. Alan must be your guardian angel."

God has guided the events of this evening and maybe even my entire life, to this moment. From my parents instilling my faith and devotion to the Blessed Mother, to my wife pushing me to retrieve a statue that has been packed beside Alan's Christmas card for years. We walk back inside and I place Alan's card on the mantle next to Mary's statue.

Gayle turns to me with a low voice, "I feel like someone is watching us. The hairs on the back of my neck are standing up. Do you feel that too?"

I tell her I'm feeling the same thing.

"Who do you think it is?" Gayle wonders, "Alan? Or some spirit?"

"I don't know. Maybe an angel, maybe Alan, or maybe it's the Holy Spirit. Whatever or whoever it is, I pray it comes from Christ.

For most of this entire year I've been in a terrible state of depression and despair over the loss of my child, even to the point of wanting to commit suicide.

When I forgave the Purgatory priest, it busted up a spiritual logjam that had blocked me off from all forgiveness, and forgiveness set the stage for recovering Mary's statue and Alan's card. Had I been immersed in bitterness and resentment, I might never have picked up on Gayle's cues, and would've completely missed out on the miraculous healing that has taken place tonight.

I'm not sure how many years Alan's card had been tucked away next to that statue of the Blessed Mother, or why I've been so worried about where he is now. It no longer matters. He's been with her all along.

CHAPTER NINETEEN

My Saturday morning church group is a source of love, support, and protection as I continue to brace against the emotional storms battering me since Alan's death. My friend Rick once told me, "We don't care if you cry, just keep coming back. I knew a guy who lost his wife, and that's all he did for six years."

Rick has extensive experience in grief counseling, and is always available to talk with me after meetings.

One day, after consoling me about Alan, he joyfully proclaims aloud, "Well, all I can say is thank God for the Resurrection!"

Two days later, Rick's Jeep overturns on the interstate an hour north of Gainesville. He doesn't survive and we are all devastated.

Rick founded our Saturday morning group many years ago. I call it "The Wulff Pack." His wit and compassion were the trademarks of a man who embodied perfectly the phrase; "Service to others." Kind and compassionate; he has helped hundreds of people and has touched all of our lives.

I had the honor of organizing Rick's memorial service at Abiding Savior Lutheran Church. So many of us needed to come together to honor him, and to show our love for him.

Thanks to my home group, I am now beginning to experience hope. Jessie comes up one weekend and returns the baseball gloves that Alan and I had played catch with hundreds of times. Her father, Armando, had gone through all of Alan's belongings stored in their attic to search for them. He understood how precious those gloves were to me. Alan and I had played catch during his last visit to Gainesville.

When Alan died, I thought he took with him any chance of me to ever experience happiness or joy again. Now I see it is a gift. Only in the darkest night of my soul could I discover a God that I can relate to—a God who knows exactly what it's like to lose a son. There *is* a Heaven, and I will see my son again. The concept of God from my Catholic childhood had to be shattered, along with the image of the angry tyrant who was ready to smash me into pieces if I stepped out of line. The pain of losing Alan has propelled me to find the real God of my understanding.

CHAPTER TWENTY

After discovering Alan's Christmas card on the anniversary of his death, I continue to feel secure, knowing that God is watching over me. Secure too, in the knowledge that Alan is in Heaven.

I continue to attend GriefShare support groups, and I stay connected to my church group and friends. When I tell Father John about Alan's card, he confirms it is definitely "a God thing."

Being moved by this miracle I've experienced, I want to share my story of despair turned into hope with anyone who'll listen. After a small church meeting one day, after sharing my story about Alan's Christmas card a woman approaches me after the meeting.

"Hi, my name is Norma. I just had to tell you that while you were sharing about your son, I felt he was communicating with me. He told me some things about you and I was wondering if you'd like to know what he said. You see I have this gift."

You'd think my past negative experiences with the occult would steer me clear of witchcraft, but the grieving process has me grabbing at any straw that offers proof of my son's safety and happiness. So, instead of bolting for the nearest exit, I leap at this opportunity to find out what message is being sent through this woman, from beyond the grave.

In a very serious tone she begins her revelation.

"Alan says you should come to our group that meets on Tuesday nights." She continues, "I also attend that group and it is there you will meet someone who will become your mentor. He will give you incredible knowledge about yourself. This will lead you to wisdom and understanding about your son's death."

Mesmerized, I ask her what else my son has communicated to her.

"I can tell he's a very sensitive soul and that he loves music, the outdoors, and that he really enjoys Tibet."

"Wait a second," I think to myself. "Enjoys Tibet?"

Alan could hardly afford to drive to *Gainesville* much less travel to Tibet. He was broke most of the time, making payments on his truck and the repair bills that went with it. A round-trip ticket to see the Dalai Lama would've cost thousands of dollars and I would've definitely been the first Alan would call on his financial-aid list. Now I'm baffled. Did he take a trip I never knew about?"

I should know better, but because Norma has accurately identified Alan's sensitive nature and his love of music, I hold fast to her words.

"Alan is desperately worried about your being so sad. You need to meet with me again tomorrow because Alan's spirit is close by and may wish to communicate further."

"Do you actually hear his voice?"

"No, it's more of a feeling that I get. You need to come back before he goes."

"Before he goes where?"

"They tend to move on. They have other things to do."

"Can you see my son? I mean does he look like he's okay? Is he with my family in Heaven?"

"He's kind of like an orb of light. He's with everyone. Catholics, Hindus, Jews—they're all orbs of beautiful light. By the way, do you have a picture of Alan?"

"I do. It's right here in my wallet." She studies it and says, "Yes, yes this is exactly how I imagine him. He's so handsome. Do you have something of Alan's like a piece of clothing, or an object that he liked? I could be more accurate if you could bring me these things. I don't need to keep them, I just need to see them."

"I have our baseball gloves and an old t-shirt of Alan's. I'll bring them tomorrow."

"Be sure you go to that Tuesday night group and remember, Alan is very concerned that you attend this group."

I'm aware that I'm completely under her spell.

Norma is not attractive. She appears disheveled and considerably overweight, but her appearance doesn't matter. She's receiving messages from my son.

The following day I go to the same meeting and show her Alan's shirt and our baseball gloves.

"Okay, this is good." She says. "This is very good."

The next Tuesday night, I show up at Norma's church group, where I'm supposed to meet my alleged mentor. The first person I run into is Renee, a woman I've known and have always liked. She also attended Alan's memorial service.

After giving me a big hug she introduces me to her partner, Kathy. Then Renee says, "I'm glad you've finally found your way to this meeting. It's special. It's also quite a coincidence seeing you here tonight, as I've been thinking about you and your son today."

"Strange," I say. "Norma guided me here after Alan somehow communicated with her, saying I'd find some kind of enlightenment here. Renee, what were those thoughts you had today about Alan?"

"I just felt he was concerned, like he wanted to say 'Please help my Dad.' All you've been doing since his death is cry at meetings."

In the following days, I begin to feel uneasy. I wonder if the information I've been given is indeed authentic. Norma's statement about Alan enjoying Tibet just doesn't jive. If she's wrong about this, what else could she be wrong about?

I call the manager of the meeting where I'd first met her, and he tells me, "She's okay. She has some serious mental problems, but basically she's harmless."

I feel so stupid. How could I not have seen this coming?

When I mention to a priest that I've had dealings with a psychic medium. I also ask if I've opened up a spiritual Pandora's box? He says, "Big time. This is why we don't deal with psychics or mediums. They're in contact with something all right, but they really don't know who or what they're in contact with."

I break off contact with Norma. My vulnerable state compromised my ability to discern fact from fiction. Now I understand how a parent who's doubled over in grief can fall prey to a variety of distractions, including those I once considered to be no more than a cheap "carnie" scam.

CHAPTER TWENTY-ONE

I'm in a Greek restaurant one day with Austin and Anna. It's the first time we've been together in Gainesville since Alan's memorial service. We talk, laugh, and have a great time. We finish our lunch and stand up to leave. As we're turning to walk out the door I suddenly call out, "Hey, hold up you guys, we gotta wait for…"

I burst into tears.

"…Bee."

For a split second I forget that he isn't with us. It's that parent thing. You know, like when you're on a vacation trip and before you pile everybody back into the mini-van, you count heads. You want to make sure you haven't left anyone behind at the rest stop on the turnpike. I stand in the restaurant lobby weeping as my kids run up to put their arms around me. They had always been Austin, Anna, and Alan—the *three* Horton children.

When people ask, "So, how many children do you have?" I use the answer Donna came up with. "I have three children—one in L.A., one here in Gainesville, and one in Heaven." It works for me because it enables me to honor Alan by keeping him included in my family.

When someone asks me, "How are you doing?" I tell them the truth. I don't do small talk anymore. Life's too short. Alan's passing established a line of demarcation in my life a time before, and a time after, I lost him. I try to make every second count now.

Susie invites me to her family's beach home on the Texas coast for the Fourth of July. This is her yearly barbecue bash in Rockport. Her husband, Bob tends his giant barbecue pit, grilling venison, steaks, and burgers. In past years, coming here had always been the highlight of our family vacations. Now, I gear up for my first celebration without Alan.

I watch the clan of cousins he spent his summers here with. They're all out in boats or on Jet Skis. He should be here, as a part of this happy entourage. But he's gone. Also gone is my sense of belonging to this treasured family tradition. It's a strange feeling, as if I'm not supposed to be here without my kids, *all* of my kids.

The annual Blue Angels air show and a mammoth fireworks display take place in front of Susie's home on the waterfront. It's one of the main reasons she'd schemed and planned for years to grab this coveted plot of real estate. I imagine Alan sitting next to me as the fireworks explode; they form majestic patterns that light up the vast Texas nighttime sky.

Bob is a cardiologist. Before leaving, I ask him a question that's been haunting me.

"Jessie said, after Alan fell from the ladder, that he jumped back up after hitting the concrete walk. She could tell by his eyes that something was terribly wrong. Was my boy in any pain?"

"Alan's jumping back up was a reflex action. Due to the nature of his brain-stem injury, I can assure you there was no pain or suffering whatsoever, especially in Alan's case. He didn't suffer. I promise you."

This is important to me, this final bit of mercy, to know he went in a flash. I tell Bob it's the way I'd like to go.

"Yeah, but unfortunately, Mikie, we don't get to choose."

Back in Gainesville, at a church meeting, a mother approaches me after I've shared about Alan.

"I'm afraid I, too, am a member of this sad fraternity," she confides, "I lost my eleven year old son in a drowning accident." I reach out and pull her to me. We both hug and cry in each other's arms. She's a stranger; yet, she's my closest sister. There's a bond between parents who've lost children, it's like no other in this world. I ask her how long ago this happened. "It's been 20 years since I lost him, and I don't think I'll ever get over it."

Every parent I share with or talk to concerning the death of a child, tells me the same thing. They will never be completely over their loss. The frequency of their pain might lessen over time, but it's still there.

If I think about Alan while I'm fishing on a beach somewhere, I'll smile. If I have to go to a dark place like the ICU ward at Ryder Trauma Center, my PTSD is going to resurrect every raw emotion. Complete closure regarding Alan may never happen in my lifetime, but at least I no longer feel guilty about my gradual reentry into a normal, happy life.

CHAPTER TWENTY-TWO

On Friday, February 24, 2012, it's Alan's birthday. He would be 27 today. I scheduled a mass for him this morning at Holy Faith. I've been staying very close to my support group this past week in anticipation of today being a sad and stressful occasion.

During mass, my grieving process is transformed from sadness to joy when Father Emmanuel draws my attention to the promise in Philippians 4:7; "And the peace of God, which transcends all understanding, will guard your hearts and minds in Christ Jesus."

Driving home from church I think of one of Alan's favorite songs, "The Lion Sleeps Tonight." Gayle returns home from the store, coincidentally singing the same tune and holding a big balloon in the shape of a lion. Anna arrives, and after dinner we write birthday notes to Alan, from all of us (including Austin's phone message), and tape them to the balloon. In a nearby field, we say a prayer and release it—watching as it soars upward into the blue cloudless sky.

We wipe away our tears as we walk back to the house. I stop to check our mailbox and find a letter from the Life Alliance Organ Recovery Agency in Miami. It seems strange to receive a response from them at this time. I've sent them several inquiries hoping to connect with any of the three organ recipients whose lives Alan saved. Unbeknownst to me, the agency had relocated their offices. It's likely none of my letters ever connected. Subsequently, I've never received a response from any of the recipients until now. It reads;

"Dear Donor Family,
My name is Carlos and I received a transplant on October 22, 2012. I am so grateful of the angel who donated their organs and who gave me my life back. If you would like to have contact with me, I would also like to have contact with you. I am thankful to the donor family for the miraculous gift and for the angel that is in Heaven that is proud of you.
I await your reply,
Carlos."

We all hug each other after reading Carlos' letter, weeping tears of joy as we realize another miracle has been bestowed upon our family.

Alan has helped to save my life too. At first I'd wanted to die, to escape the pain. I wanted to be with my "Bee," but had doubts there was such a place as Heaven. I felt that God had abandoned me.

Jessie told me Alan would get very emotional whenever he spoke of me. He had always wanted me to be happy and he worried about me getting older and dying. His death did devastate me spiritually and emotionally for a time, but I recovered from my grief. To my surprise, I find that I am stronger now than ever. My faith had to be leveled to ground zero before I could rebuild it. "Behold," St. Paul wrote in the second book of Corinthians, "all things have become new." Somehow God has used my son's death to give me new life.

CHAPTER TWENTY-THREE

Hoping to make personal contact with Carlos, I push hard for LAORA to make it happen. Months pass as my editor pressures me to send my manuscript to his publishing contact, with or without a face-to-face interview with Carlos. I hold out for as long as I can but Carlos' release information never arrives in time. After two years of waiting, I accept the fact that the interview is not going to take place. I e-mail Josie, the Family Advocate Coordinator of LAORA, thanking her for all of her efforts, and at 4:45p.m. on this rainy Tuesday, I reluctantly over-night my manuscript to a publisher in New York.

Driving home I make a mental miracle list. I'd found Alan's Christmas card and received Carlos' letter on Alan's birthday. Since I began writing this book, there have been many miracles, and tonight is no exception. After returning home from the post office, I open an e-mail from Josie. Carlos' release forms have just been delivered. I now have his Miami phone number, his address, and his written request for me to contact him.

Immediately, I call Ellis, my editor, who instructs me to e-mail his publishing contact asking her to please *not* read my manuscript, as additional and essential information has just surfaced. I add that a revised version containing an interview with Carlos, will be forthcoming by the end of summer.

Next, I call my friend Pedro who offers to set up a three-way conference call between himself, Carlos, and me. Although I'm excited, I feel unprepared for such sudden access. I ask Pedro to inform Carlos that we'll all talk tomorrow. Within minutes, Pedro calls me back.

"Mike, I have Carlos and his family on the line. They're dying to talk to you. You have to talk to them man. Don't worry, I'll translate their Spanish for you. Go ahead."

I begin conversing with Carlos in Spanish. Then, with Pedro interpreting, I talk with him, and his wife, Margarita, for the next hour. The emotional bond between Carlos and me is apparent—regardless of our language barrier. When I ask to meet with all of them in Miami for an interview, they are elated. Margarita then tells me, "Alan is our angel in Heaven. Our home is your home because you are now a member of our family."

I'm glad we're not on Skype. I wouldn't want this new family to see me crying. Before ending our conversation, Pedro tells me, "Margarita and Carlos want to prepare dinner for you. This is a very important Latin custom. You need to allow them to do this."

I tell them I'd be honored.

Pedro graciously offers to drive me down to Miami and interpret, but a family situation arises that prevents him from going. Seeking another interpreter, I contact over a dozen of my friends in Miami. No one is available to help. Carlos says his 16-year-old son, Gilberto, who speaks English, will soon be returning from the Dominican Republic. He could interpret and would also be present for family pictures.

Ellis, a trained celebrity biographer and seasoned interviewer, gives me tips on getting pertinent information. I draw up a list of 25 questions I feel are appropriate to ask Carlos and show them to Gayle. Laughing, she tells me, "These are all dumb," and throws all of them in the trash.

We write up a new list together. In the process I discover that among Gayle's many talents she'd once been a reporter for the *New York Times* for three years.

Anna agrees to do the photo shoot for me but a last minute change in her work schedule prevents her from going. I'm now left to do the drive, and the photo shoot by myself. I'm getting nervous. Gayle tells me to call my best friend Richard.

"He can help you drive and he's also a photographer."

I call Richard, explain my predicament, and ask if he'd consider going with me to the interview. There is a long uncomfortable silence. He then confesses.

"You know I have this huge issue with social anxiety. Being around strangers, and especially those who don't speak English, scares the hell out of me. Can I think about it and call you tomorrow?"

The next morning, Richard calls to tell me he wants to come along for the adventure. He's determined to work through his fear of being around people. I'm thankful for his help. Not only will I have moral and driving support, now I can turn the photo shoot over to a trained photographer.

Friday, final preparations are underway. Carlos requested a picture of Alan, so I wrap up a few I'd framed for him. Gayle packs an ice chest with sandwiches and snacks for our round-trip. After going through a final checklist, I load everything into the rental car for an early morning departure.

Saturday morning Richard and I leave at 6 a.m. Once on the highway, I hand him Alan's camera bag saying, "The manual's in here too. Think you'll have it down by the time we get to Miami?"

He replies, "No sweat, man."

I also hand him a sheet of thumbnail layouts and a list of shots we'll need to get for the book. It's obvious Richard is happy to have a camera back in his hands—photography was once his passion.

Traffic is light and switching driving duties every two hours makes the trip effortless. Eventually, the familiar skyline of Miami appears on the horizon. A great sadness begins to well up inside me. The last time I saw Miami was when Donna and I were speeding toward Ryder Trauma Center. That was more than three years ago. I still had hope then—that I was going to see my son alive.

CHAPTER TWENTY-FOUR

"Has no one returned to give praise to God except this foreigner?" Luke 17:18 NIV

I'm thinking about this passage that describes the day Christ entered a village between Samaria and Galilee. There were ten lepers entreating Him to heal them. He told them to go and show themselves to the priests. Upon doing so, they were all healed. But only one came back to thank Him. Why was Carlos the only one who thanked us? This is one of the questions I intended to ask.

Following my map, I exit off the highway into a rough neighborhood near the Miami airport, and get a few dangerous stares. I call to say I'm minutes away, and Gilberto assures me they'll be on the lookout for us.

After a few blocks, I drive up a narrow, winding street searching for his address between tall banana trees and tightly spaced trailers. "I'm getting nervous," I tell Richard. "What am I going to do when I see Carlos? What will I say?"

Carlos, a middle-aged Latin man in a brilliant blue guayabera shirt, walks out to greet us. We grab each other in a bear hug that lasts for several minutes. No words are spoken—none are needed as Gilberto, Margarita, and her brother Ynis gather around us.

Walking into their home, I notice a stalk of coconuts by the front door and wonder who had been climbing coconut trees. The inside of what I thought was going to be tight quarters for all of us turns out to be spacious and comfortable. We enter a spacious living room and begin to chat. I'm immediately aware of the warmth exuded by this family and especially the love and admiration Margarita has for her husband Carlos. They'd met when she was only 15 and he was 35. When I ask how they ended up together, Margarita says, "He just kept getting in the way of all the other men who were trying to date me."

I tell them Carlos' letter is one of the miracles that helped to inspire the rebuilding of my faith in God.

"I'd always wanted to meet the family of the angel in Heaven who gave me new life," Carlos says. "I knew that I would someday. We never lost hope that we would have that opportunity."

"I'm glad you consented," I said. "The book is unfinished until your story is added. Then, it will be complete."

We visit for nearly two hours, sharing stories about our lives, work, and children. Later, Margarita asks if we're ready to have lunch. We shift to another room with a large dining table adjacent to the kitchen where a traditional Cuban dinner of roast pork, mashed potatoes, rice, and black beans is being set out. Margarita, in a serious tone of voice, tells me, "We have Pepsi."

At first I decline, but realizing this was somehow important to them, I make sure to drink one. After saying grace, we enjoy a delicious meal followed by a colorful cake Margarita proudly serves. *Brazo Gitano*, in Spanish means "big arm," and is an internationally known Latino dessert. With it she brings out another treat in little demitasse coffee cups. My favorite—Cuban coffee, *petrolio de avion*, "jet fuel," as I fondly call it.

Setting up to record, I position Carlos and Margarita to my left, Gilberto and Ynis on my right. I stay in the middle to pass the microphone back and forth. Richard opts to float around the room shooting photos from different angles. I tell everyone this is a two-way interview, and that they are welcome to ask questions at any time.

Carlos tells me he arrived in the US in 1980 from the Dominican Republic, where he'd met Margarita. He worked hard as a truck driver and continued to work up until he fell ill in 2008. "It was then my liver quit functioning. There was very little hope but I never lost faith. I believe in miracles."

"What did Carlos have to go through to get placed on the transplant list?"

"Carlos would have these health crises where he would lose consciousness so we took him to the doctor. Because these crises were occurring closer and closer together, he needed to be placed on the waiting list immediately. There had been no prior illness or disease—my husband's liver simply quit working."

"What was the reaction of your family at the thought of losing Carlos?"

Her voice trembling with emotion, she says, "We were not happy with that news but we had hope, and we had faith in God that a miracle would take place. It did, so we first gave thanks to God, because He sent us an angel who gave me back my husband, my confidante, and a very special person in my life."

I break down mid-sentence as I'm saying, "How did you feel when the hospital called to say that they had a liver for you, Carlos?" I begin crying, as well as Carlos, Margarita, and Richard.

"It was in the middle of the night," Carlos answers. "It was a big miracle because it had been a big battle. I had been on the waiting list for a year and I'd already had two liver rejections prior to receiving Alan's. Then his liver also began to fail. They sent me home to die, but another doctor stepped in and saved me. With that doctor's help, and our prayers, we all kept fighting."

"What it's like being a father now, knowing that you're going to live?"

"It's not easy. You have to persevere and do the best you can for your kids. They can be a bit hardheaded at times. You try to correct them, but more than anything, you try to do it happily."

Gilberto says, "We go through a lot as father and son but that's because he wants the best for me. When my dad was sick we were all sad. I was the one most affected because I'm here at home all the time. When I thought he was going to die, I went into shock. The others [Carlos' two older daughters who live in Naples] couldn't be here because they live far away, but they were very worried too."

"Do you have to take anti-rejection drugs?" I ask Carlos.

"Yes. For the rest of my life."

"Carlos, your letter of thanks arrived on February 24th, 2012. That would've been Alan's 27th birthday. My son died, but because of his gift, you lived. Do you ever experience any survivor guilt?"

After Gilberto interprets my question, Carlos places his hand over his eyes. I can tell he's emotional.

"At that moment, when they told me who the donor was, I felt bad that it was a young man."

Carlos is struggling not to lose his composure so Margarita fills in for him. "I remember what my husband said when we were in the waiting room. 'If that person is alive, I don't want him to be sacrificed for me.' The nurse told me they couldn't give Carlos any more information because if they did, he might not accept the transplant. Although he was trying to take care of himself, he was also thinking of the other person who was donating this organ. The nurse did tell me that Carlos was fortunate because the donor was in excellent health. She said he was young, full of life, and very special."

Through tears, I explain, "Alan was an organ donor by choice. He wanted to save other peoples lives, and those happened to be the lives of Carlos and two others. His life wasn't taken for his organs. He died as a result of an accident. Only God knows what happened up on that ladder that day. What *is* important is that Alan's sacrifice saved lives. He would have wanted Carlos to live. Carlos, did you ever think you'd meet the family of your donor?"

"I always knew I'd meet the family because I always asked about them. I made every effort to know who Alan was. I always worried about that angel and the family that had given the authorization for his organ donation."

Margarita adds, "From the very first moment we wanted to know your family and express our gratitude. Each time I look at my husband, I see a great and beautiful act."

Gilberto says, "I'm really happy that you came here because we're already like family. I'm also thankful to Alan and to God, because now, my dad's life has been saved."

I add, "I can tell you're a good son, Gilberto."

I ask Carlos, "Alan saved three lives but you were the only one who thanked us. Why?"

"I was given back my life and my family. How could I *not* thank the family of the angel who saved me?"

Margarita adds, "As a wife, to watch your husband struggle with no hope of survival, and then, to find people so generous that they would enable my husband to return to me, left me happy. It left me with a feeling so marvelous that I will not live long enough to be able to express my gratitude."

I venture, "Since the transplant, have you had any urges to climb coconut trees or eat cream-filled pastries?"

My question is met with instant and uproarious laughter by the whole family. Ynis says, "Ha! That is too funny. He was climbing a coconut tree a week ago. He's never done that before."

Thinking back to when we first entered their home, I'd noticed the coconuts by the front door and wondered who'd been gathering them for *coco frio* [coconut milk], a favorite Latin beverage. I ask if Carlos had picked up any other acquired tastes.

"Right from the beginning, while I was still in the hospital, I had this urge to eat hamburgers, which I've never cared for. I wondered if my donor had liked hamburgers but the doctors refused to give me any information. I experienced other changes in my previous tastes and in what I desired to eat. I also wanted *dulce de manzana* [apple pie], so little by little, I began eating hamburgers and apple pie."

"God saved you for a reason Carlos. What work do you think He has in store for you?"

"I think there are many reasons God spared my life. My wife had been through so much and then she was faced with more difficulties. My prayer to God was, 'Please don't leave her alone. Help her.'"

He weeps for a moment, and then says, "I was always afraid she would be alone and what might happen to her. My children are all grown and can get on with their lives, but not her. I thought about that all the time, of her being left alone."

Wiping tears from my eyes, I say to him, "And your prayers were answered." I ask if there is anything anyone would like to add.

"More than anything," Carlos says, "I'd like to give thanks to God, because I've been able to finally meet you and to know that Alan has a great family."

Margarita adds, "We also give thanks for this opportunity to gather in our home." It is a pleasure, and as we have said before, this too, is your home. We know that wherever Alan is, he is happy, because he has such a special family and because of the lives he has saved."

After putting away my recording equipment, I ask, "Is anyone here on *Facebook* or *YouTube*?" Margarita nods. On my page we view a multitude of posts and photos of Alan. I then ask Margarita to type in: Alan Horton Life Project on *YouTube*. Up pops a video he'd done years before as a school assignment. It's a short but comprehensive look at his creativity and humor, narrated by Alan. It includes his "nude-baby picture-disc jockey-pose," as well as many of his other artistic endeavors.

With a break in the afternoon rain, Richard requests that we move outside for more shots of Carlos and the family. Afterward, I present the family with Alan's photos.

When it's time to go, a look of dismay darkens Margarita's face. "What? You're not staying with us tonight?"

"Don't worry, I'll be coming back." I invite all of them to Gainesville to meet the rest of Alan's family. They excitedly accept my offer.

We all begin hugging and saying goodbye. It's almost like Alan is here with us. I can feel his spirit and his love. I touch Carlos on the spot of where I think Alan's transplant is. I'm leaving a family I'm truly a part of. In four hours, I feel I've been with them a lifetime. Those are almost the same words inscribed on the medallion Alan was honored with by LAORA. "In Their Last Hour They Gave A Lifetime." We pull away as my new family waves goodbye.

Weeks later, in front of a large group in Gainesville, Richard comments about his interview experience with Carlos and his family.

"Never in all of my life have I ever felt the hand of God moving in such a way as it did that afternoon, while sitting at that table. I am not the same man I was."

On my desk, there is a picture of Alan and Rosie when they were 16 years old, happily entwined in a loving embrace. They appear to be very much in love. "Twin flames," as Rosie called them. There is another picture on my laptop, one of Carlos and Margarita, a middle-age couple. Obviously, they too are very much in love, dos gemellas, twin flames. Alan kept Carlos' flame burning bright for Margarita. Rosie once told me that Alan loved bringing people together. He has done just that, even in death...from one twin flame to another.

Made in the USA
Lexington, KY
09 July 2015